What Really Builds Success?

The Hidden Systems that Create Real Success in Life, Business, and Leadership

Real Success is Built Quietly—through Inner Growth that Sharpens Judgment, Strategy that Respects Reality

What Really Builds Success?

The Hidden Systems that Create Real Success in Life, Business, and Leadership

Real Success is Built Quietly—through Inner Growth that Sharpens Judgment, Strategy that Respects Reality

(Illustrated, Refined & Edited)

Gyanind

DD BOOKS
Publishers for New Generations

DD BOOKS
Publishers for New Generations

Copyright Notice for Readers

Publication Year: **2026** | Publisher: **DD Books**
ISBN: **9789372442090**

Edition: **First Edition, 2026** | Contact: ddsalesglobal@gmail.com

Book Name: **What Really Builds Success? The Hidden Systems that Create Real Success in Lifeq, Business, and Leadership**
Author: **Gyanind**
Price: **Rs 350/-**

Table of Content

Reader's Note

Most books about success promise speed. This book offers something rarer: durability.

If you have ever achieved something meaningful—only to discover that it didn't last, didn't satisfy, or didn't scale—you already understand the quiet question this book addresses. What actually sustains success once motivation fades, conditions change, and pressure increases? What allows progress to compound rather than collapse?

This book is written for readers who sense that the loud narratives of hustle, shortcuts, and overnight transformation are incomplete. It is for those who want to build lives, careers, and enterprises that work in the long run, not just perform well in brief moments of intensity. Rather than offering formulas or motivational spectacle, the chapters explore the hidden systems—psychological, ethical, strategic, and structural—that quietly determine whether effort matures into achievement or dissolves into exhaustion.

Across its chapters, the book moves deliberately between inner development and outer construction. You will encounter analyses of discipline, learning, judgment, communication, leadership, and moral responsibility—not as abstract virtues, but as operating principles that shape real outcomes. These are the mechanisms beneath success, the architecture that remains invisible until it fails. What distinguishes this work is its refusal to isolate success into a single domain. Business is examined not as a game of growth alone, but as a human system shaped by decision-making quality, ethical clarity, and adaptability. Personal development is treated not as self-absorption, but as preparation for responsibility. Leadership is framed not as authority or charisma, but as coherence between purpose and action. The chapters unfold with a widening scope. Early sections explore how individuals think, choose, and regulate themselves under pressure. Later chapters examine how those same internal systems scale outward—into teams, enterprises, institutions, and even civilizations. The lives of figures such as Bruce Lee, Nelson Mandela, and Soichiro Honda are not presented as mythology, but as case studies in disciplined practice, restraint, and long-term vision. Their significance lies not in fame, but in how they aligned belief, behavior, and consequence over time.

This book does not ask you to admire success. It asks you to understand it. It invites you to observe how momentum is built at the right speed, how learning compounds when designed intentionally, how discipline becomes freedom rather than restriction, and how influence lasts only when it is anchored in purpose.

Readers will find intellectual rigor without dryness, and reflection without sentimentality. The tone is thoughtful, grounded, and quietly demanding. It assumes intelligence, patience, and a willingness to think beyond slogans. This is not a book to skim for tricks. It is a book to live with, revisit, and apply gradually.

If you are seeking reassurance, this book may challenge you. If you are seeking clarity, it will reward you. And if you are seeking success that does not betray your values, exhaust your energy, or collapse under time, this book offers something enduring: a way to build from the inside out.

Publisher's Note

In an era saturated with advice, acceleration, and instant commentary, publishing a book like What Really Builds Success is an intentional act.

This work does not chase trends or compete for attention through exaggeration. Instead, it restores space for thoughtful reading, careful reasoning, and sustained engagement. From the publisher's perspective, this book represents the kind of writing that deserves preservation—not because it is fashionable, but because it is useful across time.

Our aim in presenting this edition has been to honor the author's voice while ensuring accessibility for modern readers. The language is reflective without being obscure, rigorous without being academic, and grounded without being reductive. The editorial approach was guided by a simple principle: clarity should never dilute depth, and readability should never compromise seriousness.

This book addresses success not as a personal trophy, but as a systemic outcome shaped by character, decision-making, environment, and ethical restraint.

It speaks to entrepreneurs, leaders, professionals, and individuals who understand that progress without structure eventually erodes. In that sense, it belongs to a lineage of works that treat human capability with respect rather than exploitation. As publishers, we are especially attentive to books that resist simplification. This manuscript does not flatten complexity into slogans. It acknowledges tension—between speed and stability, ambition and restraint, freedom and discipline. Rather than resolving these tensions artificially, it teaches readers how to navigate them intelligently.

The structure of the book reflects this philosophy. Each chapter stands independently while contributing to a coherent whole. Readers may enter from many points—business, leadership, psychology, ethics—but will find that the themes reinforce one another. This modular integrity is deliberate. It respects the way contemporary readers engage with serious nonfiction while preserving the continuity of a long argument.

We believe this book matters because it restores dignity to effort. It does not promise certainty without cost, nor confidence without competence. Instead, it affirms that learning, self-mastery, and ethical clarity are not obstacles to success—they are its foundation.

Our role as a publisher is not merely to distribute content, but to curate ideas that deserve attention. This edition has been produced with that responsibility in mind: careful formatting, thoughtful pacing, and a commitment to presenting the work as something to be returned to, not consumed once and discarded.

We invite readers to approach this book not as a manual, but as a companion in thinking. Its value will reveal itself gradually, through reflection, application, and time. That, in our view, is the highest compliment a book can earn.

Introduction

Success is often described as an outcome. This book treats it as a process that reveals itself over time.

Most narratives of achievement focus on visible moments—launches, victories, recognition, scale. What they rarely examine are the quiet decisions that made those moments possible, or the internal systems that allowed success to endure rather than disintegrate. What Really Builds Success begins where those stories usually end: beneath the surface.

At its core, this book is about alignment. Alignment between thought and action. Between ambition and restraint. Between learning and execution. Between power and responsibility. It argues that success—whether personal, professional, or institutional—is not sustained by intensity alone, but by coherence.

Readers will journey through ideas that challenge common assumptions. You will encounter success not as speed, but as rhythm. Discipline not as deprivation, but as freedom. Leadership not as dominance, but as stewardship. Growth not as expansion at all costs, but as capacity built intentionally.

The book unfolds across multiple domains. Early chapters explore how decisions compound, how momentum is built without burnout, and how individuals cultivate judgment in uncertain environments. As the narrative deepens, attention turns outward—to enterprises, leadership structures, and historical forces that shape societies. The scope widens without losing focus, always returning to the same question: what allows effort to turn into something that lasts?

Psychological insight plays a central role. Learning is treated as a system rather than a talent. Discipline is examined as an internal architecture rather than a personality trait. Communication is framed as presence and responsibility rather than persuasion alone. These themes are not presented abstractly; they are grounded in lived experience and real consequence.

The inclusion of historical and cultural figures is deliberate. Bruce Lee illustrates disciplined adaptability. Nelson Mandela embodies moral restraint under power. Soichiro Honda demonstrates patient intelligence and respect for reality. These figures are not elevated as icons, but examined as practitioners—individuals who built systems that could survive beyond their own presence.

What makes this book compelling is not suspense in the conventional sense, but recognition. Readers will recognize their own struggles with focus, direction, learning, and endurance. They will see familiar failures reframed not as personal shortcomings, but as design problems—problems that can be addressed with clarity rather than self-judgment.

The book's emotional power lies in its realism. It offers no easy answers, only understanding and careful guidance. Success is redefined as deliberate living, ethical leadership, and meaningful growth rooted in inner order. Readers are invited to build thoughtfully, with patience and reflection. Read slowly and applied wisely, the book offers a durable framework for creating a resilient life and work that can endure pressure.

Chapter-1.
The Silent Framework of Enduring Success — How thoughtful Decisions Create Businesses that Last

This chapter reveals how enduring businesses are built quietly, long before growth or recognition appears. It uncovers the hidden architecture of success—purpose, clarity, discipline, and learning—that sustains organizations over time. By focusing on thoughtful decisions rather than speed or spectacle, it offers a practical framework for building businesses that last, adapt, and earn trust.

Every enduring business begins long before revenue, recognition, or scale. It begins in a quiet moment—when a question refuses to leave the mind, when an inefficiency is noticed, or when a need is felt deeply enough to demand action. At this point, nothing is certain. There is no market validation, no guarantee of acceptance, and no visible structure to lean on. What exists instead is intent, curiosity, and the willingness to begin without applause.

In this early' stage, the most common mistake is urgency without understanding. Modern business culture often celebrates speed—launch fast, grow faster, dominate early.

Yet the businesses that truly last rarely begin with noise. They begin with attention.

Attention to the problem, attention to people, attention to constraints, and attention to the long arc rather than the immediate reward. This chapter explores that quiet beginning and the invisible structure that allows a business not merely to grow, but to endure.

Enduring success is not accidental. It is constructed patiently, decision by decision, long before outcomes become visible. The foundation of this construction is not ambition alone, but clarity. Clarity of purpose is the first and most overlooked discipline of serious enterprise. Purpose is not a slogan or a sentence framed on a wall. It is a working compass. It answers, repeatedly and honestly: What meaningful problem are we solving? Who are we truly serving? And what would be lost if we did not exist?

When purpose is clear, effort becomes coherent. Teams stop confusing activity with progress. Opportunities are evaluated not by excitement alone, but by alignment. The ability to say "no" emerges naturally—not from fear, but from focus. Businesses anchored in purpose develop a recognizable identity, one that customers and employees can feel even before they can articulate it. This identity becomes a stabilizing force during uncertainty and a guide during growth.

From purpose flows genuine customer understanding. Many organizations claim to prioritize customers, yet few are willing to truly listen to them without defensiveness.

Real customer focus requires humility—the acceptance that assumptions are often wrong and that behavior speaks more honestly than opinion. Customers reveal truth through what they repeat, where they hesitate, and what they abandon silently. These signals, when taken seriously, shape better products, clearer communication, and more resilient strategies.

Customer understanding is not a one-time exercise. It is an ongoing practice embedded into daily operations. It requires systems that surface insight, not just data. Numbers alone describe what has already happened; understanding explains why. Businesses that invest in this understanding reduce waste, improve retention, and build trust that compounds over time. Trust, once earned, lowers resistance to change and creates loyalty that marketing alone cannot buy.

Closely linked to listening is the discipline of experimentation. Sustainable businesses do not treat ideas as certainties; they treat them as questions. Each new product, feature, or process is a hypothesis waiting to be tested. Experimentation replaces reckless risk with informed learning. Instead of making large, irreversible bets, strong organizations design small, contained tests that reveal reality quickly and affordably.

This approach transforms uncertainty from a threat into a tool. Teams learn faster, adapt sooner, and build confidence rooted in evidence rather than optimism. Over time, experimentation creates a culture where learning is valued as much as winning. Such cultures remain flexible in the face of technological shifts, competitive pressure, and changing expectations—because they are built to evolve. Beneath vision and innovation lies financial clarity, the quiet discipline that determines survival. Many promising businesses fail not because their ideas lack merit, but because their finances lack understanding. Revenue without profitability, growth without cash flow, and scale without unit economics are illusions that eventually collapse under their own weight.

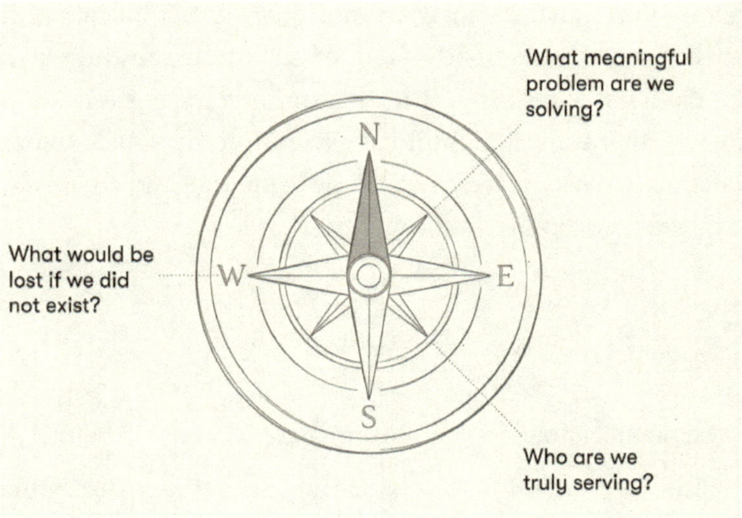

Financial discipline is not austerity. It is awareness. It requires knowing where value is created, where it leaks away, and which activities strengthen long-term health. Pricing must reflect both customer value and business sustainability. Growth must be measured not only by size, but by stability. Businesses that respect financial reality preserve choice—the freedom to invest, adapt, and endure when conditions change.

As organizations grow, operations become the bridge between intention and execution. What once worked informally no longer holds under scale. Operational design transforms strategy into repeatable action. It clarifies roles, establishes decision pathways, and ensures that work moves smoothly from idea to outcome. Well-designed operations reduce friction, prevent burnout, and create reliability without rigidity. Strong operations do not suppress creativity; they protect it. By handling routine efficiently, they free people to focus on higher-value thinking. They evolve with the organization, adjusting structure without losing purpose. Businesses that treat operations as living systems remain stable without becoming stagnant.

At the heart of every enterprise are people—not as resources, but as the living structure of the organization. Skills can be taught; character compounds. Over time, trust becomes the most valuable internal asset. Trust enables honest disagreement, shared accountability, and resilience during failure. It creates psychological safety—the condition under which learning accelerates and performance improves.

Culture is not declared; it is demonstrated. It is shaped by what leaders tolerate, reward, and model. Hiring decisions echo for years. When organizations prioritize curiosity, integrity, and adaptability alongside competence, they invest in longevity rather than convenience. Teams built on trust outperform those built on fear, even when individual talent appears similar.

Leadership, in this context, is less about control and more about stewardship. Effective leaders provide direction without arrogance and remain open to correction. They understand that authority grows stronger when paired with humility. Their role is to create conditions in which others can think clearly, act responsibly, and grow continuously.

Strategy is the discipline of choice. It is not an exhaustive plan, but a commitment to focus. Every strategic decision excludes alternatives, and this exclusion is what gives strategy power. By concentrating effort where advantage can be sustained, organizations deepen impact and conserve energy. Clear strategy aligns incentives, simplifies communication, and turns intention into action.

Marketing, when practiced well, is an act of translation rather than persuasion. It connects what a business genuinely offers with what customers truly value. Honest marketing earns trust by aligning promise with experience. When delivery reinforces messaging, reputation strengthens. When it does not, credibility erodes quickly.

Technology and data serve as amplifiers, not substitutes for judgment. More tools do not guarantee better outcomes. Insight matters only when it informs action. The most effective organizations focus on meaningful signals that guide future decisions, resisting distraction from metrics that flatter without teaching.

Reputation, though often invisible, is among the most powerful assets a business possesses. It is built slowly through everyday behavior and tested during moments of failure. How an organization responds under pressure reveals its true character. Transparency, responsibility, and visible learning preserve trust even when mistakes occur.

Growth magnifies everything. Strengths expand, but so do weaknesses. Scaling demands readiness – of systems, culture, and leadership. Expanding too early fractures foundations; expanding too late surrenders opportunity. The discipline lies in recognizing readiness and acting decisively without abandoning care.

Partnerships extend capability when grounded in mutual value. No business succeeds in isolation. Thoughtfully chosen collaborators accelerate learning, conserve resources, and open new paths. Healthy partnerships function as levers, not crutches.

Risk management preserves choice. It is not fear-driven avoidance, but thoughtful preparation. Organizations that anticipate failure modes and maintain flexibility adapt more gracefully to change. Learning organizations institutionalize reflection, capture insight, and invest in development. When curiosity fades, relevance soon follows.

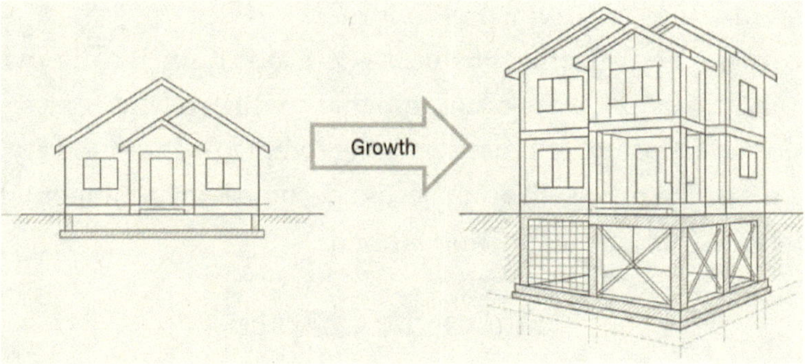

Ethical responsibility now defines legitimacy. How a business treats people, communities, and resources shapes trust and resilience. Integrity attracts customers and talent who seek alignment between values and action. Ethical constraints often spark innovation, encouraging solutions that are both sustainable and humane.

Communication binds all elements together. Clear priorities align effort; open channels surface insight. When people see their input reflected in decisions, engagement deepens. Communication is not performance—it is infrastructure. Governance protects continuity. It balances autonomy with accountability, enabling speed without sacrificing judgment. It safeguards the future while respecting the present. Above all, humility sustains longevity. Markets evolve, advantages erode, and certainty is temporary. Organizations that remain curious and adaptable avoid complacency. They honor their past without becoming imprisoned by it.

This is the quiet architecture of success. What appears sudden from the outside is almost always the result of disciplined, patient effort over time. Enduring success is not explosive; it is cumulative.

The path forward begins with attention—examining how decisions are made, where effort is spent, and what is truly learned. Build systems that support focus, trust, and learning. Treat missteps as tuition, not failure.

In the end, lasting businesses are not built by discovering secrets, but by practicing fundamentals with care and consistency. Choose purpose over noise, learning over ego, and integrity over shortcuts. Do this well, and success becomes not a moment, but a trajectory—quiet, steady, and earned.

End of the Chapter

Chapter-2. Building Momentum at the Right Speed— How to Launch Strong and Stay Adaptive in a World of Constant Change

This chapter examines the critical transition from raw momentum to disciplined adaptability. It shows how strong launches are sustained not by speed alone, but by learning systems, clear decisions, and aligned teams. By revealing how to build organizations that think, adjust, and endure, it offers a practical guide to growing with confidence in a world of constant change.

The earliest phase of a business is powered by intensity. Long hours, close involvement, and personal intuition often compensate for the absence of structure. In this stage, progress feels directly proportional to effort: work harder, push faster, solve problems as they appear. But as a venture moves from idea into reality, a quiet transformation must take place. The business can no longer rely solely on the founder's energy. It must begin to rely on the quality of its thinking.

This transition marks one of the most fragile moments in the life of a new enterprise. Many promising businesses falter here – not because the market rejected them, but because they failed to evolve from individual momentum into organizational intelligence. The pace of change is relentless. Customers adapt quickly, competitors iterate constantly, and assumptions expire faster than ever. A business that depends on heroic effort instead of collective clarity will eventually exhaust itself.

Launching strong in this environment means designing the business not just to act, but to learn. Learning must be continuous, structured, and visible. The organization itself must function as a thinking system—one that detects patterns early, challenges its own assumptions, and reallocates effort before pressure turns into crisis. This is the difference between momentum that fades and momentum that compounds.

At the core of this system lies decision-making. Every organization produces decisions, whether intentionally or by default. The strength of a business is reflected not in how many decisions it makes, but in how well it distinguishes between them. Some decisions are reversible and low-risk; others shape direction for years. Early-stage founders often treat every decision as urgent, creating cognitive overload and unnecessary conflict. Mature organizations learn to separate speed from importance.

Fast decisions should be simple, bounded, and easily corrected. Slow decisions should be rare, deliberate, and grounded in evidence. When this distinction is clearly understood, teams stop debating minor issues endlessly and focus their attention where it truly matters. Decision quality improves, fatigue decreases, and execution gains rhythm rather than urgency.

One of the most valuable disciplines in a changing world is the ability to act without pretending to know everything. Many founders feel compelled to project certainty, believing that confidence requires complete answers. In reality, false certainty creates rigidity. Markets reward responsiveness, not stubbornness. The strongest organizations move forward while openly acknowledging what remains unclear.

They design actions that generate insight rather than lock in assumptions. This ability—to delay certainty without delaying progress—creates space for learning alongside execution. Instead of waiting for perfect information, teams advance with awareness, adjusting course as reality becomes clearer. Over time, this habit builds resilience. The organization becomes comfortable operating in ambiguity without becoming reckless.

As teams expand, alignment becomes more important than agreement. Alignment is not uniform thinking; it is shared understanding of priorities. People can disagree vigorously and still move together—if they are clear on what matters most. Misalignment often hides behind polite consensus, surfacing only under pressure. Preventing this requires leaders to articulate focus repeatedly: what deserves attention now, what can wait, and what should be ignored entirely.

This clarity reduces friction not by eliminating disagreement, but by giving it a common frame. Debates become productive instead of personal. Energy flows toward progress rather than defense. Alignment, when practiced consistently, becomes a force multiplier.

Culture is often misunderstood at this stage. It is not defined by written values, benefits, or rituals. Culture is revealed through patterns of reward and tolerance. What behavior is praised? What behavior is quietly accepted? What mistakes are corrected, and which are ignored? These signals accumulate quickly, shaping how people behave when no one is watching.

If speed is rewarded but quality failures are overlooked, shortcuts will spread. If innovation is celebrated but errors are punished, experimentation will disappear. Culture is not what leaders say—it is what they reinforce under pressure. In a young organization, these signals harden rapidly. Conscious leadership is required to shape culture intentionally rather than inheriting it accidentally.

As growth increases, distance from the customer tends to widen. Founders who once heard feedback directly now rely on summaries and metrics. While abstraction is necessary, detachment is dangerous. Businesses that remain grounded design deliberate ways to reconnect leadership with customer reality. This may take the form of regular immersion, direct observation, or structured listening—not to interfere, but to recalibrate understanding.

Data explains what is happening. Proximity reminds leaders why it matters. The combination keeps intuition honest and strategy relevant.

With growth comes complexity, and complexity invites overcorrection. Many organizations respond to early disorder by introducing heavy structure too soon. Excessive rules and approvals can create a sense of control while quietly slowing learning. A more effective approach is proportional structure: add constraints only where repeated problems demonstrate necessity This keeps the organization flexible while reducing recurring failure.

Financial discipline also evolves at this stage. Early focus is on survival—understanding unit economics and maintaining cash flow. As the business stabilizes, the challenge shifts to allocation. Where should the next unit of capital go? Which investments strengthen long-term advantage, and which merely preserve comfort? Emotional attachment to past decisions can cloud judgment. Capital, like attention, must be treated as scarce and re-earned continually. Reputation forms quickly and compounds relentlessly. Organizations are evaluated not just by what they sell, but by how they behave. Consistency across all interactions—marketing, service, hiring, partnerships—creates trust that cannot be retrofitted later. Reputation is not built through messaging alone; it emerges from alignment between intention and action, especially under scrutiny.

One of the quiet strengths of disciplined organizations is optionality—the ability to choose among multiple paths as conditions change. Optionality is preserved through moderate commitments, flexible systems, diversified learning, and financial buffers. Businesses that exhaust optionality early—by overcommitting to a single strategy or identity—become brittle. When the environment shifts, they are forced into reactive decisions that undermine stability. As the organization grows, the founder's role must evolve. The founder who insists on being central to every decision eventually becomes the constraint. Effective leadership shifts from doing to enabling. It focuses on building clarity, developing others, and creating systems that scale judgment rather than authority. Letting go of control gradually, with intention, creates leverage that no amount of personal effort can match.

Hiring continues to shape the future long after the early team is formed. As scale increases, the cost of misalignment rises sharply. Technical skill remains essential, but judgment becomes decisive. Judgment shows itself in how people prioritize, handle uncertainty, and balance short-term gains against long-term consequences. Organizations that learn to assess judgment systematically build an advantage that compounds quietly.

Learning, too, must scale. Informal knowledge sharing breaks down as teams grow. Without deliberate capture of insight, organizations repeat mistakes and lose hard-earned lessons. The goal is not excessive documentation, but accessible memory—clear records of decisions, experiments, and outcomes that future teams can learn from. When learning accumulates instead of resetting, progress accelerates.

Ethical considerations deepen as influence expands. Early choices establish precedents that are difficult to reverse. Ethical alignment is not merely symbolic; it is operational. Regulations, customer expectations, and employee values increasingly intersect. Treating ethics as secondary introduces hidden costs that surface later as friction, attrition, or constraint.

Communication remains the connective tissue that holds everything together. As organizations scale, silence becomes hazardous. In the absence of context, assumptions multiply. Clear communication does not mean constant updates—it means intentional signaling of priorities, reasoning, and trade-offs. When people understand why decisions are made, even difficult choices become easier to accept.

Eventually, every business confronts the question of endurance. What does it mean to exist not just next year, but a decade from now? The answer is found less in plans and more in practice—in how learning is rewarded, how people are developed, how resources are allocated, and how conflicts are resolved. Longevity is not accidental; it is built through countless small acts of discipline and restraint.

Launching a business is not about predicting the future correctly. It is about building an organization capable of adapting intelligently as the future unfolds. The most enduring enterprises are not those that guessed right at the beginning, but those that learned fastest, adjusted earliest, and stayed anchored in purpose while remaining flexible in execution.

The rhythm of lasting progress is quiet before it is visible. It grows through clarity rather than hype, discipline rather than drama, and learning rather than certainty. Those who accept this rhythm may feel slower at first—but over time, they discover that what they are building is not fragile momentum, but durable strength.

End of the Chapter

Chapter-3.
Decoding the Quiet Mechanics of Success—The Invisible Practices that Elevate Ordinary Lives into Enduring Achievement

This chapter uncovers the quiet disciplines that transform ordinary effort into lasting achievement. It reveals success as a practiced system of habits, attention, learning, and restraint—built gradually rather than won dramatically. By shifting focus from motivation to method, it offers a practical framework for designing a life that compounds clarity, resilience, and meaningful progress over time.

Success rarely announces itself. It does not arrive with ceremony, nor does it reveal its mechanics in advance. More often, it emerges quietly—formed through repeated choices that appear insignificant in isolation but transformative in accumulation. Most lives are not changed by singular breakthroughs; they are reshaped by steady alignment between intention, behavior, and reflection. The true architecture of success is therefore subtle, built beneath the surface of daily life, where discipline replaces drama and consistency outperforms intensity.

This chapter explores success not as a destination or identity, but as a practiced condition. It rejects the mythology of sudden elevation and instead examines how ordinary people produce extraordinary outcomes through deliberate design of their days, decisions, and inner standards. What follows is not motivation, but method – a framework for living that increases the probability of meaningful success by making your life more ordered, more intentional, and more resilient over time.

The first act in decoding success is reclaiming authorship over its definition. Many people pursue goals they did not consciously choose, adopting external metrics of achievement without questioning their relevance. Money, recognition, and rank may have utility, but when they are pursued without personal alignment, they generate effort without fulfillment. Sustainable success begins with internal coherence. You must decide, explicitly, what kind of contribution you wish to make, what problems deserve your attention, and what values you are unwilling to violate in the process.

This clarity is not philosophical decoration; it is operational necessity. Without it, choices multiply unnecessarily, trade-offs feel painful, and progress becomes erratic. With it, decision-making simplifies. You gain the ability to discriminate between opportunity and distraction, growth and noise. Purpose, when articulated honestly, becomes a filter through which all commitments pass. It narrows the field of action while deepening the quality of engagement.

Once clarity is established, it must be translated into behavior. Insight without embodiment remains inert. The practical unit of success is not intention, but habit. Habits are the infrastructure of identity. They determine what you do when motivation fades and attention fractures. The most effective habits are not extreme; they are repeatable. They survive fatigue, disruption, and competing demands.

Rather than adopting an excessive number of routines, disciplined individuals focus on a small set of behaviors that reinforce their priorities. These may include consistent periods of focused work, reflective writing, physical movement, or structured learning. The specific form matters less than durability. The question is not whether a habit is impressive, but whether it persists. Over time, persistence produces capability, and capability compounds into confidence.

Attention is the next critical currency. In a world saturated with stimuli, success favors those who can allocate focus deliberately. Attention determines not only productivity, but perception—what you notice, what you value, and how you interpret experience. Editorial control over attention requires the willingness to exclude. This includes limiting informational intake, declining commitments that fragment energy, and protecting uninterrupted time for work that requires depth.

Focus should not be confused with rigidity. It is not withdrawal from the world, but fidelity to chosen aims. When attention is consistently directed toward meaningful tasks, output improves and inner coherence strengthens. The quality of work rises, and the subjective experience of time shifts from frantic motion to purposeful engagement.

Learning, when practiced well, becomes a differentiator that compounds silently. Many people consume information without integration. They read, watch, and listen continuously, yet their behavior remains unchanged. Effective learning, by contrast, is participatory. It involves testing ideas through action, observing results, and refining understanding accordingly. Learning accelerates when it is treated as an iterative process rather than passive accumulation.

Small experiments—trying a new approach, practicing a skill under constraint, or reframing a problem—produce feedback that theory alone cannot provide. Over time, this loop of action and reflection builds adaptive intelligence. It allows individuals to respond to changing conditions with insight rather than reaction.

Failure, within this framework, loses its stigma and gains utility. Failure is not evidence of inadequacy; it is evidence of engagement. The crucial distinction lies in whether failure is examined or ignored. Those who convert setbacks into learning extract long-term advantage from short-term discomfort. This requires discipline: documenting assumptions, outcomes, and adjustments with honesty. When reflection becomes routine, mistakes become instruction rather than identity.

Emotional regulation is another underappreciated dimension of success. Emotions influence judgment continuously, often without conscious awareness. Managing them does not require suppression, but recognition and timing. Mature individuals distinguish between emotions that signal values and those that merely reflect temporary states. They avoid making consequential decisions in moments of heightened emotion and cultivate practices that restore equilibrium.

Simple rituals—pausing before response, naming the emotion present, and choosing the next action deliberately—reduce the cost of impulsive behavior. Emotional discipline preserves energy for pursuits that yield lasting returns.

Relationships form the connective tissue of any successful life. Progress is rarely solitary. Networks provide information, perspective, and support during periods of uncertainty. However, valuable relationships are not transactional. They are built through consistency, generosity, and presence. Trust accumulates through small acts—reliability, thoughtful feedback, and shared effort.

Over time, such relationships create a form of social capital that extends beyond opportunity. They offer counsel during ambiguity and resilience during failure. Investing in relationships is therefore not a secondary activity, but a central strategy for long-term success. Financial stability underwrites freedom. While wealth itself is not synonymous with success, the absence of financial control constrains choice. Living below one's means, saving predictably, and investing prudently create margin. Margin enables experimentation. It allows individuals to take calculated risks, pursue learning, and recover from error without existential threat. Financial discipline is not about accumulation alone; it is about preserving optionality.

Physical health sustains cognitive and emotional performance. Without consistent sleep, movement, and nourishment, even the most ambitious plans degrade under fatigue. Treating physical well-being as foundational rather than auxiliary produces dividends across all domains. Small, consistent investments in health yield disproportionate returns in clarity, patience, and endurance.

Rituals provide continuity in the midst of variability. They reduce decision fatigue and signal priorities through action rather than intention. A simple morning or evening ritual—structured reflection, planning, or decompression—anchors identity over time. Rituals are not rigid constraints; they are stabilizing references that maintain direction amid change.

Risk, properly understood, is not an enemy. It is an inherent feature of any meaningful pursuit. Intelligent risk management involves identifying potential failure modes, creating safeguards, and maintaining reserves—emotional, financial, and relational. This approach preserves agency when outcomes diverge from expectation. Decision-making improves when it is designed. High-stakes decisions benefit from structure: time delays, alternative generation, dissenting perspectives, and predefined review points. This architecture reduces the influence of bias and emotion. Good decisions are not merely decisive; they are well-processed. Curiosity becomes productive when disciplined. Unstructured curiosity fragments attention, while focused curiosity builds expertise. Selecting domains worthy of sustained inquiry and investing in them consistently transforms interest into mastery. Over time, this depth produces insight that distinguishes contribution from commentary.

Narrative coherence shapes both internal resilience and external credibility. How you interpret your own story influences persistence. Integrating setbacks into a larger arc allows experience to inform direction rather than undermine confidence. A coherent narrative does not deny difficulty; it contextualizes it. Selective refusal is essential. Every commitment excludes alternatives. Those who succeed over the long term practice deliberate constraint, preserving energy for work that compounds. Saying no, when done respectfully, protects future capacity.

Creativity flourishes under constraint. Limits force prioritization and synthesis. Time, scope, or resource constraints channel imagination into problem-solving rather than diffusion. Meaningful work often emerges not from freedom without bounds, but from creative pressure within chosen limits.

Mentorship accelerates growth when approached with humility and reciprocity. Seek guidance from those who have navigated similar terrain, but adapt lessons rather than imitate paths. Effective mentorship evolves into mutual respect and shared inquiry.

Sustained performance requires renewal. Periods of rest and reflection are not indulgences; they are maintenance. Without renewal, effort degrades into repetition. With it, clarity and creativity are restored.

Integrity compounds quietly. Reliability, honesty, and fairness generate trust that opens doors long after initial effort is forgotten. Integrity reduces friction and attracts collaboration.

Humility anchors progress. Recognition of limits preserves adaptability. Those who remain open to correction continue to grow; those who cling to certainty stagnate.

Success, understood correctly, is not a spectacle. It is the cumulative outcome of ordinary practices executed with care, patience, and moral seriousness. Design your life around a small number of coherent commitments, defend them against distraction, and allow time to do its work. In doing so, you build not only achievement, but a form of success that endures—quietly, steadily, and by design.

End of the Chapter

Chapter-4.
Forging the Backbone of Enterprise—The Human Craft Behind Lasting Micro, Small, and Medium Business Success

This chapter illuminates the quiet human craft that sustains micro, small, and medium enterprises. It reveals how judgment, care, and ethical restraint—not scale or spectacle—form the backbone of lasting business success. By focusing on people, discipline, and contextual understanding, it offers a grounded framework for building enterprises that endure, serve communities, and grow with integrity.

When economic progress is discussed, attention often drifts toward scale: multinational corporations, disruptive technologies, and global markets. Yet beneath these visible structures lies a quieter, more durable foundation. Micro, small, and medium enterprises form the connective tissue of real economies. They are not peripheral actors; they are the steady engines that translate aspiration into livelihoods, innovation into service, and community needs into practical solutions. Their success is not accidental, nor is it mechanical. It is human work, shaped by judgment, restraint, patience, and care.

The strength of a small or medium enterprise does not come from size or spectacle. It comes from backbone. Backbone is the ability to remain coherent under pressure, ethical under constraint, and adaptive without losing identity. It is forged gradually through daily choices that prioritize sustainability over shortcuts and learning over display. This chapter examines how that backbone is built—through human craftsmanship applied to commerce.

Every viable enterprise begins with an honest encounter with reality. Before strategy, branding, or scale, there is a problem that someone experiences repeatedly and intensely enough to seek relief. Successful entrepreneurs resist the temptation to start with solutions. Instead, they begin by dwelling in the problem—understanding its context, frequency, and emotional weight. They ask not only what is broken, but why it matters in the life of the person experiencing it.

This depth of understanding cannot be outsourced or rushed. It requires proximity to customers, sustained observation, and humility. In micro and small enterprises, this proximity is often a natural advantage. Founders speak directly with customers, witness friction firsthand, and experience the consequences of their decisions immediately. Those who use this closeness to learn rather than defend assumptions develop insight that no market report can provide. From this understanding emerges the craft of solution-making. In the world of small enterprises, success rarely comes from novelty alone. It comes from appropriateness. Solutions must fit the context—culturally, economically, and practically. A product that is slightly better made, a service that is more respectful, or a process that removes confusion can outperform more sophisticated alternatives because it integrates seamlessly into daily life.

Quality, in this setting, is not excess. It is reliability. Customers return not because they are dazzled, but because they are understood.

Trust forms when expectations are met consistently. Over time, this trust becomes the enterprise's most defensible advantage. Early execution must remain disciplined. One of the most common errors in small business formation is overbuilding—adding features, offerings, or complexity before demand is proven. Sound enterprise-building resembles skilled craftsmanship: test the material, shape gradually, and respond to resistance rather than forcing form prematurely. Small, usable versions of an offering reveal far more truth than polished but untested visions.

Feedback, especially when uncomfortable, is the teacher here. Enterprises that treat early criticism as information rather than insult develop resilience. They learn to refine instead of retreat, adjust instead of abandon. Over time, this posture transforms uncertainty from a threat into a source of direction.

Financial clarity is inseparable from survival. In micro and small enterprises, cash flow is not an abstract metric—it is continuity. Understanding how money moves through the business determines whether commitments can be honored and growth sustained. Many ventures fail not due to lack of demand, but due to financial opacity. When costs, margins, and timing are poorly understood, even growing businesses become fragile.

Pricing deserves particular care. It communicates value, confidence, and respect. Prices that are set too low signal insecurity and starve the enterprise of reinvestment capacity. Prices set without regard to customer reality alienate those the business intends to serve. Thoughtful pricing balances fairness with sustainability, enabling the enterprise to invest in people, quality, and learning.

Operations translate intention into consistency. In early stages, informal coordination may suffice, but growth exposes its limits. Repeated errors, confusion, and dependency on specific individuals signal the need for operational structure. Good operations are not bureaucratic; they are humane. They reduce cognitive load, clarify responsibility, and prevent avoidable stress. Processes should exist to serve people, not the reverse. The aim is not rigidity but reliability—systems that support quality even when conditions are imperfect. When operations are thoughtfully designed, they free human attention for judgment, creativity, and care.

People are the living core of any enterprise. In small organizations, each hire has disproportionate influence. Skill matters, but character matters more. Curiosity, accountability, and willingness to learn determine whether a team becomes adaptive or brittle. Alignment around values and standards creates cohesion that cannot be enforced through rules alone.

Leadership, in this environment, is relational. It is demonstrated through presence, consistency, and fairness rather than authority. Effective leaders in small enterprises set clear direction while remaining open to revision. They protect focus, address problems early, and model the behaviors they expect. Their influence shapes culture not through speeches, but through everyday conduct.

Marketing for small and medium enterprises is not amplification; it is articulation. It clarifies what the business stands for and why it exists. The most effective communication resonates because it is honest. It reflects lived experience rather than aspiration alone. When marketing promises align with delivery, credibility compounds naturally.

Technology offers leverage, but only when chosen deliberately. Digital tools can extend reach, simplify operations, and enhance customer experience. Yet complexity introduced prematurely becomes a liability. Each tool should earn its place by reducing friction or increasing clarity. Technology should strengthen relationships, not replace them. Reputation accumulates quietly. It is shaped by how an enterprise responds when something goes wrong, how it treats customers who complain, and how it honors commitments when it would be easier not to. Over time, reputation becomes a form of capital—reducing marketing costs, attracting better partners, and creating resilience during downturns.

Growth requires discernment. Expansion without preparation strains systems, culture, and finances. Healthy growth follows demonstrated demand, operational readiness, and cultural stability. Scaling should feel deliberate rather than frantic. It should preserve what made the enterprise viable in the first place while extending its reach.

Partnerships amplify capability. Few small enterprises succeed alone. Suppliers, collaborators, and community institutions form ecosystems that distribute risk and accelerate learning. The most valuable partnerships are grounded in mutual benefit and clear expectations. They extend strength without creating dependency.

Risk management is not pessimism; it is respect for reality. Disruptions—financial, operational, or external—are inevitable. Enterprises that anticipate them maintain flexibility. Diversified revenue, adaptable processes, and strong relationships create optionality. Optionality preserves agency when circumstances shift. Learning sustains relevance. Enterprises that capture insight—documenting decisions, experiments, and outcomes—build memory. This memory prevents repetition of avoidable mistakes and accelerates onboarding of new team members. Learning becomes an institutional habit rather than an individual burden. Ethical conduct strengthens enterprise durability. Decisions about sourcing, labor, transparency, and community engagement shape trust. Enterprises that integrate values into operations reduce long-term risk and attract aligned customers and employees. Ethics are not constraints; they are stabilizers.

Communication aligns effort. Internally, clarity prevents drift and resentment. Externally, it sets accurate expectations. Silence creates ambiguity, and ambiguity breeds mistrust. Consistent, honest communication sustains alignment as complexity increases. Governance protects continuity. As enterprises mature, decision rights, accountability, and oversight must be clarified. Good governance balances autonomy with coherence, enabling agility without erosion of purpose.

Humility completes the backbone. Markets evolve, customer needs change, and certainty decays.

Enterprises that remain curious rather than defensive adapt more readily. Humility allows learning to continue long after early success.

What appears from the outside as sudden success is usually the visible result of countless invisible acts: listening carefully, choosing restraint over impulse, correcting course without fanfare, and honoring commitments repeatedly. This is the human craft of enterprise.

For those who undertake this journey, the reward is not only economic. It is agency—the ability to create value with dignity, to serve real needs, and to shape work that respects both people and reality. This backbone is not inherited. It is built—slowly, deliberately, and with care—through the everyday craftsmanship of meaningful enterprise.

End of the Chapter

Chapter-5.
When Time Becomes Leverage—How Experience, Even Late in Life, Compounds into Lasting Enterprise

This chapter challenges the myth that enterprise belongs only to the young, revealing how time, experience, and judgment become powerful forms of leverage. It shows how businesses started later in life gain strength through clarity, restraint, and relevance. By treating experience as an asset, it offers a grounded path to building enterprises that endure, serve real needs, and compound steadily over time.

There is a persistent myth in modern culture that innovation belongs to the young and that enterprise is a race best entered early. This belief is both shallow and historically inaccurate. Many of the most resilient, well-loved businesses were built not by those chasing speed, but by those who possessed judgment. Time, when lived attentively, does not diminish entrepreneurial capacity—it refines it. Experience becomes leverage when it is applied with intention, patience, and humility.

Beginning or rebuilding a business later in life is not an act of desperation; it is often an act of clarity. By this stage, illusions have worn thin. There is a sharper sense of what matters, a reduced appetite for vanity, and a deeper understanding of trade-offs. These qualities are not abstract virtues; they are practical assets. They reduce waste, prevent impulsive decisions, and anchor enterprise in reality rather than aspiration alone. The foundation of any durable business, regardless of the founder's age, is relevance. Relevance emerges from lived understanding of human problems. Those who have spent decades working, raising families, managing households, and navigating institutions carry with them a quiet encyclopedia of unmet needs. These are not speculative opportunities; they are frictions encountered repeatedly over time. Businesses built around such problems begin with an advantage: the founder understands the customer not as a demographic, but as a person.

Starting later often means starting with fewer illusions about scale. This is a strength. Small beginnings allow ideas to be tested without catastrophic risk. They create space for adjustment and learning. A modest offering that works reliably is more powerful than a grand vision that collapses under its own complexity. When an enterprise is small, the feedback loop is tight. You see how people respond, where they hesitate, and what they return for. This intimacy with reality accelerates improvement.

Progress in such ventures is rarely dramatic. It arrives as consistency: showing up daily, delivering what was promised, correcting errors promptly, and listening carefully. Over time, this reliability differentiates the business. Customers return not because they are dazzled, but because they trust. Trust is not built through advertising alone; it is built through repetition of care.

Capital discipline is particularly important when beginning later. The objective is not rapid expansion, but sustainability. Limited resources enforce focus. They compel founders to ask essential questions: Will this expense generate learning? Will it strengthen the core offering? Will it preserve flexibility? Every decision must earn its place. This discipline protects against common failures—over-hiring, premature marketing, or excessive inventory driven by optimism rather than evidence.

Financial stability also preserves dignity. It allows entrepreneurs to make decisions without panic, to negotiate fairly, and to endure slow periods without sacrificing standards. A simple reserve, conservative spending habits, and diversified income streams extend runway. Runway, in turn, preserves choice. Choice is the real currency of freedom.

Optionality deserves deliberate cultivation. Optionality is the ability to pivot without collapse. For a business, it may take the form of multiple suppliers, flexible delivery channels, or complementary offerings that share infrastructure. For individuals, optionality comes from maintaining skills, relationships, and modest financial buffers. Enterprises that preserve optionality are less brittle. When conditions change, they adjust rather than react.

Marketing in later-life enterprises is most effective when grounded in honesty. Clear language outperforms hype. Say plainly what you do, who you serve, and why it matters. Stories drawn from real customer experiences communicate value more credibly than slogans. Word-of-mouth remains unmatched, especially in community-centered businesses. It is earned through consistency, responsiveness, and small acts of generosity that signal care.

Technology can extend reach without diluting humanity—if chosen carefully. Digital tools should simplify, not complicate. Basic systems for payments, record-keeping, and customer communication reduce friction and free time for relationships. The goal is not automation for its own sake, but clarity and reliability. Technology should serve trust, not obscure it.

Operations are the quiet enablers of quality. Simple routines—inventory checks, service scripts, delivery protocols—prevent avoidable errors. These systems do not limit creativity; they protect it. When basics are handled reliably, attention can shift to improvement rather than correction. Over time, operational clarity transforms effort into leverage.

People matter disproportionately in small enterprises. Each collaborator shapes culture. Hiring for character—dependability, curiosity, integrity—creates cohesion that skills alone cannot provide. In close-knit teams, trust compounds quickly. Conflicts are resolved faster, learning spreads organically, and resilience increases. Leadership, in this context, is practiced rather than proclaimed. It is visible in how decisions are made, how mistakes are handled, and how people are treated under pressure. Effective leaders create coherence. They protect standards without rigidity and invite input without surrendering direction. Their authority emerges from consistency rather than control.

Pricing must honor both value and sustainability. Undervaluing work erodes morale and limits reinvestment. Overpricing alienates core customers. Thoughtful pricing reflects cost, quality, and service while remaining aligned with customer reality. Tiered offerings can balance accessibility with margin, allowing the business to serve diverse needs without dilution.

Compliance and legality deserve early attention. Clear registration, tax understanding, and record-keeping prevent later disruption. This administrative discipline is not a burden; it is protection. It preserves credibility and reduces the likelihood that success will be undermined by preventable errors. Community relationships amplify impact. Partnerships with local organizations, suppliers, and peer businesses extend reach and credibility. These relationships function on reciprocity. Shared initiatives, referrals, and collaboration distribute risk and accelerate learning. A business embedded in its community is more resilient than one that stands apart. Feedback should be welcomed systematically. Simple questions—what worked, what didn't, what would help—surface insight. Acting on feedback demonstrates respect. Customers who see their input reflected become advocates. Advocacy compounds faster than advertising.

Growth must be paced. Scaling amplifies both strengths and weaknesses. Before expanding, ensure economics are stable, processes are repeatable, and culture can absorb complexity. Growth pursued prematurely strains trust and reputation. Growth pursued deliberately preserves them.

Legacy becomes more salient later in life. Many founders care deeply about what their enterprise represents. Decisions about sourcing, labor practices, and environmental impact shape that legacy. These choices may slow short-term gains but strengthen long-term reputation and alignment.

Sustainable work rhythms are essential. Longevity requires rest, boundaries, and renewal. A business that consumes its founder is not a success. Designing work that supports health, relationships, and joy is not indulgence; it is strategic.

Mentorship accelerates learning. Seeking counsel from those who have navigated similar paths reduces avoidable mistakes. Equally, offering mentorship strengthens the ecosystem and deepens one's own understanding.

Risk management is foresight in action. Identifying vulnerabilities and preparing contingencies reduces surprise. Diversification, insurance, and reserves do not eliminate risk; they preserve agency when risk materializes.

Progress deserves recognition. Celebrating milestones sustains morale and reinforces identity. These markers create a narrative of momentum that carries the enterprise through uncertainty. Ultimately, age reframes ambition. It shifts focus from spectacle to substance, from speed to steadiness. Enterprises built later in life often endure because they are grounded in reality, guided by judgment, and shaped by care. They demonstrate that success is not a function of starting early, but of starting wisely.

This chapter offers no guarantees. It offers something more durable: a way of thinking that treats experience as advantage, restraint as strength, and consistency as compounding force. When small, thoughtful actions are repeated over time, they produce enterprises that serve real people, generate real value, and stand quietly against the erosion of time.

End of the Chapter

Chapter-6.
The Unseen Route to Real Success—Moving Beyond Hustle into Purpose-Driven Entrepreneurship

This chapter challenges the hustle-driven narrative of entrepreneurship, revealing a quieter and more durable path to success. It explores how purpose, judgment, and disciplined learning replace exhaustion with alignment. By shifting focus from constant motion to meaningful direction, the chapter offers a framework for building enterprises that endure—grounded in relevance, guided by humility, and sustained by intentional practice.

Modern culture celebrates visible effort. Long hours, relentless grind, public sacrifice, and constant motion are treated as proof of seriousness. Yet when we examine enterprises that truly endure—those that survive volatility, earn trust, and contribute meaningfully—we find that their success rarely follows the loudest path. It follows a quieter route, one shaped less by force and more by alignment. This chapter explores that unseen route: a form of entrepreneurship rooted not in exhaustion, but in purpose, judgment, and disciplined adaptation.

Purposeful entrepreneurship begins with a redefinition of ambition. Ambition is often misunderstood as speed or scale, when in truth it is direction. Without direction, effort dissipates. Purpose gives effort shape. It answers the question of why before rushing toward how. Entrepreneurs who operate from purpose are not immune to hard work, but their work is oriented—it builds toward coherence rather than scattering energy across reactive pursuits.

At the center of this orientation is a fundamental recognition: markets do not reward intensity; they reward relevance. A business succeeds not because the founder wants it badly enough, but because it addresses a real need in a way people recognize as valuable. Purposeful entrepreneurs therefore begin not with their vision, but with reality. They study the everyday experiences of the people they hope to serve, seeking to understand where friction persists, where dignity is compromised, and where effort is wasted.

This form of inquiry requires restraint. It demands the discipline to delay attachment to a solution until the problem is fully understood. Entrepreneurs who rush to implementation often mistake activity for progress. Those who pause to interpret context—observing how people behave rather than how they describe behavior—gain insight that shapes more resilient ventures. They learn that unmet needs often express themselves indirectly, through workarounds, repeated complaints, or resigned acceptance rather than explicit demand.

Listening, in this sense, is a form of analysis. It is not passive absorption but structured attention. Purposeful entrepreneurs treat assumptions as provisional. They design small tests to validate understanding, gathering evidence from action rather than opinion. When early efforts fall short, they respond not with defensiveness, but with curiosity. Each misalignment becomes instruction.

This posture transforms failure. Instead of being an emotional verdict, failure becomes directional information. When founders detach personal identity from specific outcomes, they retain the flexibility to learn. The enterprise evolves not by avoiding error, but by metabolizing it. Over time, this adaptive rhythm builds strategic confidence grounded in experience rather than optimism.

A defining feature of purposeful entrepreneurship is patience with learning curves.

Hustle culture emphasizes acceleration; purposeful practice emphasizes accumulation. Learning compounds when it is allowed to settle into practice. Entrepreneurs who build enduring ventures recognize that insight gained too quickly often lacks depth. They favor progress that is measured, documented, and integrated.

Decision-making within this framework becomes intentional. Not all decisions require the same urgency or depth. Some are reversible and benefit from speed; others carry long-term consequences and demand reflection.

Entrepreneurs who distinguish between these categories preserve mental energy. They act quickly where learning is cheap and slow down where commitment is costly. This discrimination prevents both paralysis and recklessness.

Resources—time, capital, and attention—are treated as instruments rather than trophies. Purposeful entrepreneurs resist the temptation to raise or spend money prematurely. Capital, without clarity, amplifies confusion. Instead, resources are deployed in service of learning. Small, focused investments test assumptions and reveal constraints. Each resource earns its place by contributing to understanding or sustainability.

Value creation, in this context, is rhythmic rather than episodic. Many ventures invest heavily in launch moments, expecting momentum to carry forward. Yet customers experience value through repetition.

Reliability, responsiveness, and consistency define trust. Purposeful entrepreneurs design for these rhythms. They ensure that everyday interactions reinforce expectations rather than undermine them. Over time, this consistency becomes reputation.

Entrepreneurship is inseparable from psychology. The internal narratives founders carry shape how they interpret challenge. When difficulty is framed as personal inadequacy, progress stalls. When difficulty is framed as structural signal, learning accelerates. Purposeful entrepreneurs cultivate emotional literacy—not to eliminate emotion, but to contextualize it. They allow feelings without letting them dictate strategy.

Humility is central to this process. It is not modesty, but openness. Humble entrepreneurs remain alert to new information, even when it contradicts prior beliefs. They invite critique without surrendering direction. This balance—conviction paired with receptivity—creates cultures where learning outpaces ego. Leadership emerges as a relational craft rather than a command structure.

Even solo entrepreneurs lead—through example, discipline, and the standards they uphold.

As teams form, leadership becomes the work of alignment. Purposeful leaders articulate direction clearly, model behavior consistently, and create environments where others can contribute meaningfully. Authority is earned through coherence rather than control.

Narrative competence strengthens this alignment. People need to understand not only what a venture does, but why it exists and how it intends to grow.

Purposeful entrepreneurs communicate with clarity and restraint. Their stories are not embellished; they are integrated. These narratives help customers, partners, and employees situate themselves within the enterprise's trajectory.

Systems support scale without eroding humanity. As ventures grow, memory and informal coordination fail. Purposeful entrepreneurs introduce lightweight systems—simple processes, clear roles, and transparent communication—that preserve quality without creating rigidity. Systems exist to reduce friction, not to replace judgment.

Ethical practice is embedded, not advertised. Decisions about pricing, labor, transparency, and community impact are guided by values expressed in action. Purposeful entrepreneurs recognize that ethical shortcuts create hidden liabilities. Integrity, practiced consistently, reduces friction and attracts alignment over time. Risk is engaged thoughtfully. Purposeful entrepreneurs do not seek certainty before acting, nor do they gamble indiscriminately. They structure risk into manageable experiments. Each bet is bounded, reviewed, and aligned with long-term intent. This approach preserves optionality—the freedom to adjust course without collapse.

Time management reflects value hierarchy. Not all tasks deserve equal attention. Purposeful entrepreneurs prioritize work that strengthens the core: understanding customers, improving delivery, developing people, and reflecting on direction. Urgency does not automatically trump importance. Renewal is scheduled, not postponed, because endurance depends on it. Cultural intelligence deepens relevance. In diverse markets, understanding how people interpret value, trust, and communication shapes design and delivery. Purposeful entrepreneurs adapt without losing identity. They integrate perspective rather than impose uniformity. Psychological endurance sustains the journey. Entrepreneurship unfolds unevenly. Confidence rises and falls. Purpose provides continuity during fluctuation. Reflection, community, and self-care anchor engagement. Endurance is not stoicism; it is sustained participation with perspective.

Ultimately, entrepreneurship is not a quest for escape or domination. It is a disciplined relationship with reality. Purposeful entrepreneurs accept constraints, learn from resistance, and build within context. They measure success not solely by growth, but by coherence—between intention and impact, effort and outcome. This hidden path does not promise ease. It promises durability. It replaces frantic motion with directed movement, replaces spectacle with substance, and replaces exhaustion with meaning. Those who walk it may progress quietly, but they build enterprises that last—because they are grounded in understanding, guided by purpose, and sustained by disciplined practice.

End of the Chapter

Chapter-7.

Build What Endures—The Quiet Principles that Turn Effort into Businesses that Truly Work

This chapter distills the quiet principles that separate durable businesses from fleeting success. It reveals how focus, consequence awareness, disciplined learning, and integrity turn effort into enterprises that truly work. By replacing noise with judgment and speed with clarity, it offers a practical framework for building businesses that remain resilient, trusted, and effective across cycles of change.

In every era of commerce, advice multiplies faster than understanding. Each cycle produces its own vocabulary—growth hacks, automation stacks, viral loops—promising leverage without depth. Yet when the noise recedes and outcomes are measured over time, a different pattern emerges. The businesses that work—those that survive shocks, retain trust, and generate steady value—are rarely built on cleverness alone. They are built on judgment. They endure because they focus on what matters, ignore what does not, and repeat a small number of sound practices with care.

This chapter is about those practices. Not as slogans, but as working principles. It argues that durability in business comes from restraint as much as ambition, from listening as much as acting, and from choosing substance over spectacle. What follows is a framework for building enterprises that function well—not just in favorable conditions, but across cycles of uncertainty.

The first principle is consequence awareness. Every organization is flooded with tasks, signals, and requests. The difference between progress and exhaustion lies in the ability to distinguish between activity and consequence. Consequential work is work that meaningfully alters outcomes. It improves customer retention, reduces failure rates, strengthens economics, or deepens capability. Non-consequential work may feel urgent, but it rarely changes direction.

Leaders who build what endures develop a habit of asking a simple question: If this is done well, what changes? If the answer is vague or cosmetic, the work is likely noise. Consequence awareness is not about doing less; it is about concentrating effort where it compounds. Over time, this concentration creates asymmetry—small teams achieving outsized impact because their energy is directed rather than dispersed.

From consequence flows focus. Focus is not intensity; it is coherence. In environments saturated with interruption, sustained attention becomes a strategic asset. Enduring businesses institutionalize focus through structure, not heroics. They design calendars that protect thinking time, meetings that exist for decisions rather than updates, and communication norms that respect deep work. When focus becomes cultural rather than individual, quality rises and errors fall—not because people work harder, but because they think more clearly.

Listening is the next quiet discipline. Businesses fail not from lack of intelligence, but from misinterpretation of reality. Listening in this context is not the passive collection of opinions; it is the disciplined study of behavior. What do customers repeat? Where do they hesitate? What do they abandon without complaint? These patterns are more honest than surveys and more valuable than anecdotes. Organizations that listen well treat customers as co-designers of value. They seek clarity rather than confirmation. They ask precise questions and observe outcomes closely. When feedback contradicts internal beliefs, they revise beliefs rather than argue with evidence. This posture prevents drift and keeps offerings grounded in lived need rather than internal narrative.

Experimentation translates listening into action. Where uncertainty exists—and it always does—small, structured experiments reduce risk and accelerate learning. Effective experimentation isolates the most fragile assumption, defines success criteria in advance, and commits to a decision point. The purpose is not to prove competence, but to uncover truth. Over time, repeated experimentation builds an internal map of what works and why. Financial clarity anchors this process. Without understanding unit economics, even the most admired products become liabilities. Enduring businesses know where money is made, where it is lost, and why. They track acquisition costs, retention behavior, and margin stability with discipline. These numbers are not constraints on creativity; they are signals that guide it.

Spending follows learning. Capital is deployed not to impress, but to discover. Investments are tied to questions that matter: Will this channel retain customers? Will this improvement reduce churn? Will this process lower error rates? When spending is aligned with learning, waste declines and confidence increases. Growth becomes intentional rather than accidental.

Culture shapes execution long before strategy does. Culture is revealed in moments of pressure—how mistakes are handled, how dissent is treated, and how success is attributed. Enduring organizations reward clarity, honesty, and responsibility. They create space for disagreement without fear and accountability without blame. Rituals such as retrospectives, shared reviews, and open post-mortems convert experience into memory.

Leadership in this environment is not theatrical. It is architectural. Leaders define priorities, clarify trade-offs, and remove friction. They design decision pathways so routine choices do not consume attention. They model humility by seeking disconfirming evidence and changing course publicly when warranted. This behavior creates psychological safety, which in turn accelerates learning.

Technology serves strategy, not the reverse. Tools amplify intention, but they also amplify confusion when adopted prematurely. Enduring businesses choose technology that simplifies, integrates, and remains replaceable. They avoid building dependency on systems that outpace their maturity. Technology decisions are guided by customer experience and operational reality rather than novelty.

Marketing reflects truth. It is a translation of value, not an invention of it. Businesses that last align promise with delivery. They test messages with the same rigor they test products, scaling only what produces retention rather than attention alone. Early customers are treated as sources of insight and credibility, not merely revenue. This alignment builds trust that compounds through reputation rather than spend.

Operations preserve trust through consistency. Customers forgive occasional failure; they do not forgive unpredictability. Simple processes—clear onboarding, quality checks, complaint resolution—create reliability. As volume grows, these processes must be made explicit to prevent drift. Operational discipline is not bureaucracy; it is respect for the customer's experience.

Partnerships extend capability when chosen deliberately. Strong partnerships are based on complementary strengths and shared incentives. They are tested in small increments, measured honestly, and expanded cautiously. Partnerships increase optionality when aligned and drain energy when they are not.

Risk management preserves choice. Enduring businesses do not attempt to eliminate uncertainty; they design resilience. Diversified suppliers, conservative cash buffers, and flexible contracts create room to maneuver. Scenario thinking reveals vulnerabilities early and informs preparation. The goal is not prediction, but readiness.

Learning becomes an organizational habit when captured. Decision journals, experiment logs, and shared reflections create institutional memory. This memory allows teams to move faster without repeating mistakes. Over time, learning itself becomes a competitive advantage because it compounds silently and cannot be easily replicated.

Humility sustains progress. Markets change. Customers evolve. What worked once may fail again. Organizations that treat success as final become fragile. Those that treat it as provisional remain adaptive. Ambition remains important, but ambition grounded in evidence endures longer than ambition fueled by belief alone.

If there is one posture that defines businesses that work, it is this: they operate as systems of deliberate learning guided by consequence, focus, and integrity. They replace frantic motion with measured progress. They do not chase relevance; they earn it. Build what endures. Do fewer things with greater care. Listen more than you declare. Learn faster than you commit. When these principles shape daily practice, success ceases to be mysterious. It becomes the predictable outcome of thoughtful work repeated over time—and that is the quiet power behind enterprises that truly work.

End of the Chapter

Chapter-8. The Architecture of Conviction—How Women Transform Belief into Enduring Enterprises

This chapter explores how women transform belief into a practical architecture for lasting enterprise. It reveals belief not as emotion, but as discipline—shaped into systems, judgment, and relationships over time. By examining how empathy, clarity, learning, and purpose are translated into durable structures, the chapter offers a grounded model of entrepreneurship that endures through coherence rather than spectacle.

Belief is rarely dramatic. It does not announce itself with noise or spectacle, nor does it demand immediate recognition. Yet belief is one of the most powerful economic forces in human history. It shapes judgment before evidence is complete, sustains effort when results lag behind labor, and quietly governs how risk, responsibility, and opportunity are interpreted. For the women whose entrepreneurial journeys inform this chapter, belief was not a single emotional surge or a moment of confidence—it was a disciplined, ongoing practice. A way of thinking, choosing, and acting long before external validation appeared.

This chapter examines belief not as motivation, but as infrastructure. It explores how belief is translated into systems, habits, decisions, and relationships—and how, over time, those structures give rise to enterprises that endure. These are not stories of sudden breakthroughs or mythologized success. They are studies in accumulation: of insight layered upon insight, of judgment refined through repetition, and of enterprises built patiently before they were visible or celebrated.

At the beginning of every entrepreneurial path lies a fundamental divide: the difference between an idea and a contribution. Ideas are abundant; contribution is rare. The women examined here crossed that divide by resisting the temptation to chase novelty for its own sake. Instead, they returned repeatedly to a grounding question: What persistent problem exists in the real lives of real people—and why am I positioned to understand it deeply? Their answers emerged not from abstraction, but from observation: unmet needs encountered firsthand, inefficiencies noticed through lived experience, and frustrations voiced quietly but consistently by others.

This orientation reveals a crucial truth about enterprise: relevance matters more than originality. Businesses succeed not because they are new, but because they are necessary. Deep relevance is born of empathy—not as sentiment, but as perception. Empathy, in this context, is an operational skill. It requires attentive listening, the suspension of assumptions, and the discipline to notice patterns that others dismiss as ordinary. Several women described discovering their core opportunity not through formal research, but through informal conversations, repeated complaints, and overlooked inconveniences that revealed systemic gaps. Listening, over time, became strategy.

From empathy emerges clarity. Clarity about whom the business serves, what value it creates, and why it exists beyond profit. Purpose, as these entrepreneurs practiced it, was not decorative language reserved for mission statements. It functioned as a decision-making compass. When growth created complexity and options multiplied, purpose provided coherence.

It guided choices about product design, pricing ethics, hiring standards, partnerships, and expansion. Purpose was not static; it was revisited, tested, and refined—but it always remained anchored in real impact rather than abstract aspiration.

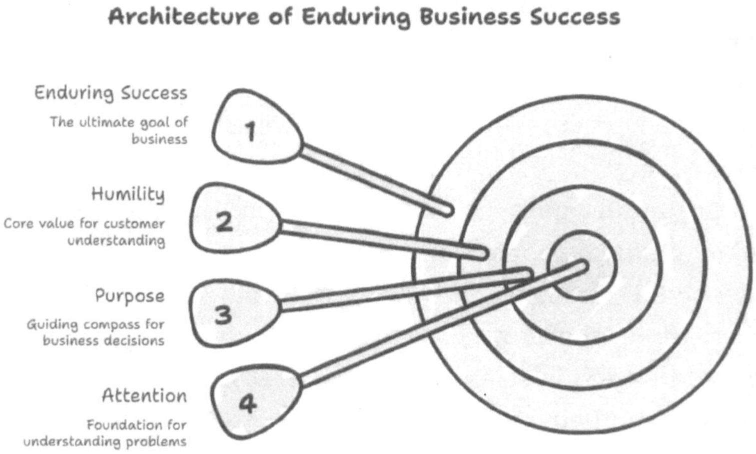

As ventures moved beyond inception, belief faced its first serious test: the necessity of systems. Inspiration initiates action, but systems sustain it. Ideas can inspire excellence once; systems make excellence repeatable. The women in this chapter spoke extensively about the deliberate transition from personal effort to structured processes. They built workflows that reduced dependence on individual heroics, established quality standards that protected customer trust, and created feedback loops that allowed learning to compound. One founder described this shift as the moment when "values stop being intentions and start becoming behavior." In this framing, belief is encoded into process.

Financial understanding emerged as another decisive layer of maturity. Passion alone does not preserve enterprises; precision does. These entrepreneurs learned to treat financial literacy as a core leadership responsibility, not a secondary task to be delegated blindly. They developed fluency in unit economics, cash flow dynamics, pricing discipline, and capital allocation. Financial clarity allowed them to distinguish between growth that strengthens foundations and growth that erodes them. Importantly, they rejected the false opposition between purpose and profitability, recognizing that sustainability requires both. Financial discipline, for them, was an ethical practice as much as a technical one.

Decision-making evolved alongside scale. In early stages, urgency governs choices; speed compensates for limited information. As complexity increases, however, discernment becomes critical. These women articulated a nuanced approach to judgment: separating decisions that are reversible from those that are defining. Experiments were encouraged where learning was cheap and recoverable. Identity-shaping commitments—governance structures, cultural norms, long-term partnerships—were approached with deliberation. This balance preserved agility without sacrificing integrity, allowing adaptation without erosion of core principles.

Leadership, as practiced by these entrepreneurs, departed sharply from the archetype of solitary authority. Leadership was understood as an enabling function rather than a controlling one. Their focus shifted from directing outcomes to designing environments in which others could perform at their best. This required clarity of expectations, consistency in communication, and a feedback culture rooted in respect rather than fear Authority was exercised through trust and structure, not proximity or dominance. In such environments, responsibility distributed itself naturally, and organizational resilience increased.

A persistent theme across these enterprises was a deep commitment to learning. Markets, customers, and technologies generate continuous feedback; thriving organizations know how to listen to it. The women institutionalized learning through regular reflection, customer dialogue, performance metrics, and post-action analysis. Mistakes were treated as data rather than personal failure. Over time, this orientation produced a compounding advantage: faster adaptation, sharper judgment, and reduced defensiveness. Learning, in this sense, was not episodic—it was cultural.

Equally important was narrative competence. Enterprises exist within stories—told to customers, employees, investors, and communities. These women developed the ability to articulate not only what their businesses did, but why they existed and where they were going. Their narratives were not exaggerated promises; they were coherent explanations of intent, grounded in honesty. By translating complexity into meaning, they allowed stakeholders to align emotionally and intellectually with the enterprise. A strong narrative did not obscure uncertainty—it contextualized it.

The relational fabric of business proved decisive. Trust emerged as a form of invisible capital, accumulated slowly through consistency and reliability. Early relationships—often built within local communities or personal networks—became the foundation for reputation and growth. Trust reduced friction, accelerated adoption, and created resilience during inevitable setbacks. Unlike financial capital, trust compounds through use rather than depletion. It transforms transactions into partnerships and customers into advocates.

Negotiation, viewed through this relational lens, became an exercise in alignment rather than extraction. These entrepreneurs rejected adversarial models that prioritize short-term gain over long-term viability. They approached negotiation as a collaborative design process—seeking agreements that balanced interests and preserved dignity. This approach expanded opportunity, reduced conflict, and strengthened ecosystems around their ventures.

Risk was never eliminated, but it was reframed. Rather than avoiding uncertainty, these women learned to manage exposure through experimentation, diversification, and contingency planning. They accepted that perfect foresight is unattainable, and built organizations capable of absorbing surprise without collapse. Resilience replaced prediction as the primary defense against volatility.

Identity, including gender identity, shaped these journeys in complex ways. The women neither ignored nor overstated its influence. Instead, they treated identity as context—one that informed perspective, empathy, and leadership style. Rather than framing gender solely as obstacle or advantage, they integrated lived experience into strategic insight, allowing it to sharpen perception without constraining possibility.

Sustainability—personal and organizational—emerged as a non-negotiable principle. These entrepreneurs rejected cultures that glorify exhaustion. They designed rhythms of work that protected health, relationships, and cognitive clarity. Endurance, they understood, is a strategic asset. Enterprises built for the long term require leaders who can think clearly over decades, not merely sprint through moments.

Expectation management played a subtle but critical role. Early wins and losses alike were contextualized within trajectory rather than treated as verdicts. Progress was measured by learning velocity and coherence of direction, not by isolated milestones. This steady calibration preserved psychological stability and reduced reactive decision-making.

As enterprises scaled, leadership transformed again—from centralized control to distributed authority. Values, language, and systems replaced proximity as coordinating mechanisms.

Autonomy was encouraged within clearly defined boundaries, allowing organizations to grow without fragmentation.

Adaptability remained constant throughout. Change was not treated as interruption, but as environment. By sensing shifts early and testing responses incrementally, these women engaged change proactively rather than defensively. Adaptability, practiced consistently, became a source of opportunity rather than disruption.

Ultimately, impact defined success. These enterprises mattered because they contributed beyond themselves—creating livelihoods, improving access, solving meaningful problems, and shaping healthier systems. Profit sustained the mission, but contribution justified it.

This chapter offers no shortcuts. What it presents instead is a pattern: belief practiced as discipline, empathy translated into structure, learning embedded into culture, and purpose aligned with action. When repeated patiently over time, these practices generate enterprises with quiet gravity—businesses that do not merely exist, but endure, influence, and matter.

End of the Chapter

Chapter-9.

Designing the Inevitable—Seven Silent Disciplines that Turn Effort into Certainty

This chapter reveals how success can be engineered rather than hoped for. It introduces seven quiet disciplines that transform scattered effort into reliable outcomes by aligning attention, learning, judgment, and relationships. Instead of chasing intensity or luck, readers gain a practical system for making progress predictable—turning uncertainty into structure and sustained achievement into an inevitable result of disciplined practice.

Success almost never announces itself with fireworks. It grows quietly, shaped by choices that appear ordinary in the moment but prove decisive over time. What separates consistent achievers from those who rely on bursts of luck is not talent alone, nor motivation, nor even intelligence—it is the presence of an internal system. A way of thinking and acting that steadily converts intention into outcome. This chapter is about that system.

Here, success is not treated as an abstract ideal or a reward reserved for a fortunate few. It is treated as a consequence—one that can be made increasingly predictable when certain skills are practiced with discipline. These skills are not loud. They do not trend easily or offer instant gratification. Yet they quietly restructure how attention is used, how uncertainty is handled, and how progress compounds. When cultivated together, they make success less a matter of chance and more a matter of design.

The first discipline is precision of leverage. Most people pursue success by accumulating tasks. They equate effort with volume, believing that doing more will eventually produce results. In reality, progress is rarely democratic; a small number of actions create the majority of impact. Precision begins by shifting the question from What do I want? to What action most influences the outcome I care about? This is the leverage question. It forces clarity by eliminating the comfort of busyness. Instead of spreading attention thinly across dozens of initiatives, it demands focus on the few moves that meaningfully alter direction. When leverage is clear, energy stops leaking into low-return activity, and learning accelerates because cause and effect become visible.

The second discipline is learning through controlled action. Ambition often collapses under uncertainty because people wait for confidence before acting. But confidence is rarely a prerequisite for progress; it is often a byproduct of testing. Controlled action takes the form of small, intentional experiments. Each experiment is built around an assumption, a risk, and a measurable signal. The goal is not to prove oneself right, but to reduce ignorance quickly and cheaply. By treating action as inquiry rather than commitment, fear loses its grip. Over time, these small tests accumulate into judgment—judgment grounded not in theory, but in lived evidence.

The third discipline is the stewardship of attention. Attention is the medium through which all meaningful work occurs, yet it is routinely treated as expendable. When attention is fragmented, even high effort produces shallow results. Stewardship begins with recognition: not all hours are equal, and not all tasks deserve equal mental clarity. Protecting attention means designing days and weeks around cognitive priorities rather than reactive demands. It means reserving uninterrupted space for thinking, limiting unnecessary interruptions, and establishing personal rules that reduce decision fatigue. This is not about rigid schedules, but about respect for mental energy. When attention is protected, insight becomes more frequent, decisions become cleaner, and work regains depth.

The fourth discipline is structured learning from others. Feedback, when left to chance, is often vague or emotionally charged. When designed intentionally, it becomes one of the fastest engines of improvement. Structured learning involves asking better questions, at better times, to better sources. Instead of asking whether something is liked, it asks where confusion arose, what alternatives were considered, and what caused hesitation. Just as important is responding visibly to feedback—showing how insight was translated into adjustment. This practice transforms feedback from judgment into collaboration. Over time, it builds trust and dramatically shortens the distance between effort and refinement.

The fifth discipline is economic clarity as a thinking tool. Many people treat financial understanding as a technical necessity rather than a strategic lens. Yet clarity around costs, trade-offs, and value creation sharpens nearly every decision. Economic clarity does not require complex forecasting; it requires knowing which variables truly matter and tracking them honestly. When decisions are framed in terms of opportunity cost—what must be sacrificed to pursue a given path—choices become grounded. This discipline replaces hopeful guessing with informed judgment and prevents momentum from being built on fragile assumptions.

The sixth discipline is relationship cultivation with intent. Progress rarely unfolds in isolation. Insight, opportunity, and resilience are often transmitted through relationships. Intentional relationship-building is not transactional networking; it is stewardship. It involves showing up consistently, contributing without immediate expectation, and being clear about needs without entitlement. Strong relationships act as amplifiers: they surface blind spots early, provide access to knowledge, and extend credibility beyond individual effort. Over time, a well-tended network becomes an ecosystem in which progress accelerates naturally.

The seventh discipline is emotional regulation in service of judgment. Resilience is often misunderstood as toughness or emotional suppression. In practice, its true function is to preserve clear thinking under pressure. Setbacks are inevitable; what matters is whether they distort perception or generate learning. This discipline is built through simple but powerful habits: reviewing outcomes objectively, slowing down irreversible decisions, and restoring mental capacity through rest and reflection. Emotional regulation allows individuals to remain engaged with reality rather than reacting defensively to it. It ensures that difficulty becomes a teacher rather than a derailment.

These disciplines do not operate independently. They form a system. Precision of leverage directs experimentation. Experiments generate feedback. Feedback refines judgment. Attention stewardship creates the space for reflection. Economic clarity anchors ambition. Relationships expand perspective. Emotional regulation preserves learning across setbacks. When practiced together, they transform effort into momentum and momentum into consistency.

Application begins with restraint, not overhaul. Observe one week of work honestly. Identify where attention is scattered and where leverage is unclear. Remove or constrain a single recurring distraction. Choose one assumption worth testing and design a small experiment. Clarify one economic question that influences your next decision. Reach out to one person with genuine curiosity or support. These steps are modest, but they initiate alignment.

Measurement should remain purposeful. Metrics are valuable only insofar as they inform better action. Choose indicators that illuminate progress toward leverage, not those that merely signal activity. When measurement clarifies learning, adjustment becomes swift and ego loses influence.

Rituals sustain progress when motivation fluctuates. Brief daily reviews, weekly reflection on experiments, and periodic recalibration of goals create continuity without rigidity. Over time, these rhythms shape identity. You become someone who learns systematically, adjusts calmly, and acts deliberately. Generosity quietly reinforces the entire system. Contributing insight, time, or support without immediate return builds trust and expands possibility. It transforms individual effort into collective momentum and ensures that success does not isolate but connects.

There is no single formula for achievement. Paths differ, contexts vary, and definitions of success evolve. Yet these seven disciplines form a durable foundation. They are learnable, repeatable, and adaptable across domains. When practiced consistently, they replace unpredictability with structure and anxiety with method.

Begin with one discipline. Practice it simply. Then add another. As these quiet skills compound, success no longer feels accidental. It becomes the natural consequence of a life and work system designed to learn, focus, and endure.

End of the Chapter

Chapter-10. Becoming by Design—Lessons from a young Maker on How to Shape a Life with Intention

This chapter explores how an intentional life is built through everyday acts of making, choosing, and refining. Drawing lessons from a young maker's mindset, it shows how curiosity becomes judgment, failure becomes insight, and work becomes meaningful craft. The value lies in learning to see the world as editable—and taking responsibility for shaping it with clarity, care, and purpose.

There are ideas that do not arrive loudly. They enter quietly, settle slowly, and then begin to reorganize how you see your work, your choices, and your sense of responsibility. Such ideas rarely come packaged as grand theories. More often, they surface as simple observations spoken plainly—ideas that feel obvious only after they have changed you. This chapter is built around that kind of thinking. Not as a tribute to a famous figure, but as an exploration of a way of becoming: how a person learns to see possibility where others see permanence, how standards are formed, how failure is metabolized into judgment, and how work becomes an extension of meaning rather than a mere transaction of time for reward.

The central premise is deceptively modest: much of the world around us—tools, systems, conventions, and institutions—was created by ordinary people responding to constraints. Once this is understood, reality no longer feels immovable. It becomes editable. This realization carries two consequences. The first is freedom: you are not required to accept the world exactly as you inherit it. The second is obligation: if things can be changed, then the quality of change matters. The work of becoming begins at this intersection—between possibility and responsibility.

To live as a maker is to develop the habit of seeing systems rather than surfaces. It means asking how things work, why they were built that way, and where they fail the people who use them. This orientation does not require extraordinary intelligence; it requires curiosity paired with persistence. Competence is built by touching the material of the world—by studying processes, attempting small constructions, and learning through friction. Over time, repeated contact with reality produces not just skill, but judgment. Judgment is what allows a person to distinguish between what merely functions and what truly fits.

From judgment emerges taste. Taste is often misunderstood as preference or aesthetic flair. In practice, it is a disciplined standard. Taste helps you choose among many viable options by clarifying what is worth doing well and what is worth refusing altogether. Developing taste requires patience. It demands exposure to work that endures beyond trends and restraint from premature conclusions. Taste is formed slowly, through comparison, revision, and reflection. It governs not only what you create, but how you choose collaborators, define scope, and decide when something is finished. Importantly, taste is inseparable from constraint. Limits sharpen clarity. By deciding what not to include, you give form to what truly matters.

A defining feature of meaningful work is that it seeks to be felt, not merely used. Functional solutions address problems; resonant creations form relationships. When a piece of work respects the time, attention, and dignity of those who encounter it, it earns trust. This trust compounds. It cannot be manufactured through persuasion alone; it is produced through coherence and care. Small details—clarity of language, thoughtfulness of interaction, reliability of performance—signal intent. They communicate whether the maker values the human experience on the other side of the work. Over time, these signals create attachment that outlasts convenience or novelty.

Failure occupies a central role in this process, but not in the way it is often celebrated. Failure is neither a badge of honor nor a private shame. It is information. What determines its usefulness is the posture taken toward it. Learning from failure requires emotional steadiness and intellectual honesty. It requires separating the outcome of an attempt from the worth of the person making it. When failure is examined calmly—assumptions identified, signals interpreted, decisions revised—it becomes a tool for refinement. Organizations and individuals who normalize this kind of examination accumulate competence rapidly because mistakes are converted into shared understanding rather than buried or dramatized.

Another essential shift in the work of becoming is the integration of life and work into a coherent narrative. This does not mean erasing boundaries or glorifying overwork. It means choosing pursuits that can sustain meaning over time. Short-term rewards are easy to calculate; long-term coherence is harder but more consequential. Work that teaches transferable skills, builds durable relationships, and aligns with evolving values preserves optionality. It allows a person to grow without becoming trapped by momentum alone. When decisions are evaluated through this lens, trade-offs become clearer and regret becomes less likely.

Simplicity emerges as both a technical and ethical discipline. Making something simple is not superficial reduction; it is the result of deep understanding. Complexity must be mastered before it can be responsibly removed. True simplicity reduces cognitive burden, lowers the likelihood of error, and respects the user by not asking them to compensate for poor design. In systems, simplicity creates resilience. In products, it builds trust. In life, it clarifies priorities. The discipline of simplicity resists accumulation for its own sake and insists on alignment between purpose and execution.

These principles coalesce into a repeatable method. First, observe carefully. Pay attention to how people actually behave, not how they claim to behave. Notice friction, workarounds, and quiet dissatisfaction. Second, prototype modestly. Make ideas concrete enough to encounter reality without overcommitting resources. Third, learn honestly. Treat outcomes as signals rather than verdicts. Fourth, refine relentlessly. Edit without sentimentality. Remove what does not serve the core. Finally, scale with care. Growth should amplify quality, not dilute it. Scaling before coherence is established multiplies flaws rather than value.

Leadership within this framework is an act of stewardship. It involves protecting standards in moments when compromise would be easier, defending time for reflection when urgency pressures speed, and resisting metrics that reward appearance over substance. Durable organizations are not built on continuous acceleration, but on rhythms that allow quality to stabilize before expansion. Pauses are not failures of ambition; they are investments in alignment.

Responsibility runs through every stage of this process. When you shape tools, systems, or ideas that affect others, you influence daily life in ways both visible and unseen. Responsible making anticipates downstream effects, prioritizes dignity, and reduces harm through thoughtful design. This is not abstract morality; it is practical foresight. Work that is ethically considered early tends to be more robust, more adaptable, and more trusted over time.

For those seeking to apply these ideas, the path begins small. Observe a familiar environment and identify a friction others have normalized. Attempt a modest improvement. Share it. Watch what happens. Revise. Protect time to reflect on what you are learning. Establish personal standards and hold to them even when shortcuts are tempting. Ask not only whether something works, but whether it improves the experience of those who encounter it.

These practices do not eliminate uncertainty. Even the most disciplined makers encounter setbacks and public failure. What they eliminate is arbitrariness. They replace guesswork with method and transform aspiration into a daily craft. The deeper argument of this chapter is not about achievement, but about authorship. A life shaped by intention is not one free of difficulty; it is one in which difficulty is engaged thoughtfully. You do not need permission to begin shaping the world you inhabit. You need attention, patience, and the willingness to take responsibility for what you build. This is the work of becoming – not the pursuit of legend, but the steady practice of leaving your work, your systems, and your life more coherent, more humane, and more meaningful than you found them.

End of the Chapter

Chapter-11.
The Living Voice— How Clear Speech Becomes Trust, Presence, and Influence

This chapter reveals how voice becomes a living instrument of trust, presence, and influence. It shows that clear speech is not performance, but alignment—between breath, body, intention, and ethics. Readers gain practical insight into how thoughtful voice cultivation deepens credibility, strengthens relationships, and turns everyday communication into a powerful force for leadership and shared understanding.

Every voice carries a history before it carries a message. Long before listeners analyze words, they register tone, rhythm, and intent. A voice can steady a room or unsettle it, invite cooperation or provoke resistance, signal care or indifference. To speak so that people want to listen is not a theatrical skill reserved for performers; it is a human craft that shapes leadership, learning, and relationships. This chapter explores that craft in full—how voice emerges from the body, how meaning travels through sound, and how speech becomes an ethical bridge between thought and action.

The living voice is not about dominance or persuasion through force. It is about alignment: between breath and intention, between words and values, between speaker and listener. When that alignment exists, speech feels less like transmission and more like exchange. People listen not because they must, but because they sense that listening will reward them with clarity, respect, and usefulness. Voice begins before language, in physiology. Breath is the unseen architecture of speech. A shallow, hurried breath constricts phrasing and conveys urgency even when none is intended. A grounded breath, drawn fully and released steadily, gives the voice range and calm authority. This is not a metaphor; it is mechanical. Breath supports sound, and sound shapes perception. A person who speaks from a settled breath communicates composure even in disagreement. Developing this foundation does not require dramatic training—only regular attention. A few minutes each day spent breathing slowly, expanding the lower ribs, and extending the exhale conditions the nervous system to support clear expression under pressure.

Posture follows naturally from breath. The body is the instrument through which voice resonates. When posture collapses, sound thins and confidence leaks. When posture is rigid, sound hardens and warmth disappears. The most effective posture is neither performative nor casual; it is balanced. Weight grounded, chest open without tension, neck free. Such alignment allows sound to travel and signals self-respect without aggression. Listeners respond to this equilibrium instinctively. They may not consciously notice posture, but they feel its effects in how safe or strained the interaction becomes.

Tone—the emotional color of the voice—emerges from preparation rather than personality. Many people believe they are "stuck" with a particular voice, but tone is shaped by habits of resonance and articulation. A voice warmed through gentle humming, slow vowel shaping, and deliberate consonants gains texture and approachability. Warmth does not mean softness; it means fullness. A full tone carries authority without intimidation. Over time, this quality becomes associated with reliability. People begin to trust not just what is said, but how it sounds. Pitch variation gives speech contour. Monotony erases hierarchy within ideas; everything sounds equally important, which makes nothing memorable. Natural pitch movement helps listeners navigate meaning. Slight rises suggest curiosity or openness. Falls signal completion or gravity. Purposeful emphasis directs attention without demanding it. Learning to vary pitch consciously—marking where energy lifts and where it settles—turns speech into a guided experience rather than a stream of information.

Pace determines whether ideas land or evaporate. Speech that rushes overwhelms; speech that drags anesthetizes. Effective pacing respects the listener's processing capacity. Complex ideas require space. Important ideas require pause. Silence, when used intentionally, is not emptiness but invitation. It gives listeners permission to think, to absorb, to prepare a response. Many speakers fear silence because it feels like loss of control. In reality, silence is a form of control—the kind that builds trust rather than tension.

Clarity is the ethical core of good speech. To be clear is to respect the listener's time and cognitive effort. Clarity grows from clean articulation and disciplined language. It favors concrete nouns over abstractions, verbs over qualifiers, structure over improvisation. This does not mean avoiding complexity; it means translating complexity into sentences that the ear can follow. Spoken language lives differently than written language. It needs shorter units, stronger emphasis, and audible signposts. A clear speaker anticipates confusion and resolves it before it appears.

Story gives speech memory. Human beings are wired to retain meaning when it is carried by experience. A brief, specific episode—a moment of decision, a small mistake, an unexpected outcome—can anchor an abstract idea in lived reality. Effective stories do not exaggerate; they illuminate. They are chosen not for drama but for relevance. Ethical storytelling honors truth and context. It uses narrative to clarify stakes, not to manipulate emotion. When story serves understanding, it deepens connection rather than distorting judgment.

Authenticity is not performance; it is congruence. Audiences sense when words and inner state diverge. A speaker who claims certainty while betraying tension in breath and pitch undermines credibility. Authentic voice accepts imperfection. It allows space for uncertainty without surrendering authority. Preparation enables this honesty. When you know your material deeply, you can speak flexibly and admit limits without fear. Candor, offered responsibly, builds confidence faster than polish alone.

Listening is the invisible half of speaking. The most compelling speakers are responsive, not rehearsed in isolation. They notice facial cues, shifts in posture, changes in energy. They adjust in real time—slowing when confusion appears, simplifying when attention wavers, inviting questions when resistance surfaces. Speaking well is a conversation, even in formal settings. A single sincere question can transform a monologue into a shared inquiry. When people feel included in meaning-making, their attention strengthens.

Practice is indispensable, but its quality matters. Repetition without reflection hardens habits rather than refining them. Purposeful practice isolates variables: pacing, emphasis, clarity, filler words. Recording oneself and listening critically reveals patterns invisible from the inside. Silence can replace verbal tics. Pauses can replace urgency. Over time, practice builds muscle memory that holds under stress, freeing attention for connection rather than self-monitoring.

Anxiety deserves respect, not denial. Nervousness is the body's signal that something matters. Attempting to eliminate it often backfires. Rituals work better. A short breathing sequence, a familiar warm-up, a private review of the opening line—these routines create predictability that steadies physiology. With repetition, the body learns that speaking is not threat but engagement. Anxiety softens into alertness.

Words carry moral weight. Metaphors frame reality; labels shape behavior. Thoughtful speakers choose language that clarifies rather than inflames, that humanizes rather than reduces. This does not require blandness. It requires care. Precision in language sharpens thinking and expands choice. When persuasion is necessary, it should invite consent, not bypass judgment. Ethical speech respects autonomy by presenting evidence, acknowledging limits, and making trade-offs visible.

Influence rests on three foundations: credibility, clarity, and connection. Credibility grows from steadiness and competence.

Clarity from structure and articulation. Connection from warmth and relevance. Voice is the medium through which these qualities travel. When aligned, they create influence that feels earned rather than imposed.

Progress comes from structure. Build simple routines that reinforce development: regular vocal warm-ups, weekly reflection on conversations that went well or poorly, brief preparation checklists before important discussions. Track meaningful signals: Did people ask better questions? Did misunderstandings decrease? Did someone respond by changing their mind or behavior? These indicators reveal impact more reliably than applause.

Physical presence completes the picture. Movement, when intentional, reinforces meaning. A step forward can signal emphasis; stillness can signal gravity. Gestures clarify scale and sequence. Excess movement distracts, but purposeful movement punctuates thought. Space is part of communication. Proximity can soften hierarchy and invite dialogue when used with sensitivity. Cultures of good speech depend on cultures of good listening. Model the behavior you want to hear. Summarize others' points before adding your own. Ask what matters most to be understood. Create moments where devices are absent and attention is shared. These practices raise the collective standard of communication and make every voice more effective.

Over time, your voice becomes part of your professional and personal identity. It is how ideas travel ahead of you and how trust lingers after you leave the room. This identity is not fixed; it evolves with attention and care. The most compelling voices are not inherited; they are cultivated.

In the end, speaking so that people want to listen is an act of respect. It treats attention as a gift and returns it with usefulness. It recognizes that influence is not about overpowering others, but about making shared understanding possible. When voice is practiced with that ethic, it becomes more than sound. It becomes a medium for thoughtful action, collective judgment, and humane leadership.

End of the Chapter

Chapter-12.
The Learnable Mind—How Skill is Built Faster than Belief Allows

This chapter dismantles the myth that learning is reserved for the gifted or naturally disciplined. It reveals skill-building as a practical, repeatable system—one that replaces fear with method and belief with evidence. Readers gain a clear framework for learning faster, breaking skills into manageable parts, and transforming discomfort into progress through deliberate practice and intelligent design.

One of the most quietly damaging ideas in modern culture is the belief that learning belongs to the gifted, the young, or the unusually disciplined. We tell ourselves stories about talent as if it were destiny, about intelligence as if it were fixed, about mastery as if it required a lifetime of suffering before any reward appears. These stories sound rational, even scientific, but their real function is psychological: they protect us from the discomfort of beginning. They give us permission not to try.

The truth is less dramatic and far more empowering. Learning is not a mystery. It is a system. A repeatable sequence of choices about attention, practice, feedback, emotion, and environment. When those choices are aligned, progress accelerates. When they are not, even years of effort produce little movement. This chapter is about replacing myth with method—about showing how learning actually works in practice, and how ordinary people can acquire new skills far faster than they imagine, without extraordinary talent or heroic willpower.

Most people do not fail to learn because they are incapable. They fail because they misunderstand what learning feels like in its early stages. Early learning is awkward. It is inefficient. It exposes ignorance. These sensations are often misinterpreted as signals of inadequacy, when in fact they are signals of engagement. The mind resists this phase because it threatens identity: no one enjoys feeling incompetent. But competence is never the starting point. It is the byproduct of deliberate contact with difficulty.

A more useful way to approach learning is to abandon the fantasy of mastery and aim instead for usefulness. The critical threshold is not excellence; it is functionality. How long does it take to become good enough to use the skill in a real context, to receive feedback, to feel the first signs of agency? That threshold is far closer than most people believe. Once usefulness is reached, learning stops being abstract. It becomes experiential. Progress becomes visible. Motivation shifts from fragile hope to earned confidence.

The first step in accelerating learning is intelligent decomposition. Skills are rarely singular. They are composites—bundles of smaller abilities working together. When learners treat a skill as a monolith, they feel overwhelmed. When they break it into parts, they gain traction. Consider any complex ability: writing, programming, speaking, playing an instrument, managing people. Each contains sub-skills that can be practiced independently. Decomposition transforms an intimidating goal into a series of manageable tasks and reveals where effort should be concentrated first.

Decomposition also reveals leverage. Not all sub-skills contribute equally to early progress. Some unlock functionality faster than others. Identifying these high-leverage components is a strategic act. It prevents wasted effort on refinements that matter later and focuses attention on what creates immediate capability. Learning accelerates when effort is sequenced rather than scattered.

Once a skill is broken down, the learner must acquire just enough understanding to self-correct. This is a crucial inflection point. Many people linger too long in passive consumption—reading, watching, planning—without ever entering the feedback loop. Information without action feels productive, but it produces no correction. Correction is the engine of learning. To self-correct, you need a rough mental model of what good performance looks like. This model does not need to be perfect. It needs to be usable. Examples, demonstrations, and simple criteria are sufficient. With a basic model in place, practice becomes informative rather than repetitive.

The third accelerator is barrier removal. Learning does not fail because people lack discipline; it fails because friction accumulates. Tiny obstacles—setting up tools, finding materials, choosing what to practice—compound into avoidance. Intelligent learners redesign their environments so practice becomes the path of least resistance. They reduce decision-making, shorten setup time, and make practice visible and convenient. This is not motivation; it is mechanics. When barriers are low, consistency becomes natural.

Consistency matters because learning is not linear. It depends on repeated exposure spaced over time. Short, frequent sessions often outperform occasional marathons because they allow the brain to consolidate patterns incrementally. This leads to the fourth principle: focused practice over a meaningful threshold. There is a point—often reached within a few dozen hours of deliberate effort—where confusion gives way to pattern recognition. Errors become more specific. Adjustments become more precise. At this stage, learning becomes self-sustaining. The skill begins to reward attention rather than punish it.

Deliberate practice is not mere repetition. It is structured engagement with improvement as the goal. Each session targets a specific weakness or sub-skill. Feedback is immediate or quickly obtained. Adjustments are intentional. Without feedback, practice is motion. With feedback, it is education. Recording oneself, tracking outcomes, comparing attempts, or seeking targeted input turns effort into information.

A decisive psychological shift occurs when mistakes are reframed as data. Inexperienced learners experience errors as personal failures. Effective learners experience them as signals. Errors locate the boundary of current ability. They show where effort will pay off next. This reframing changes emotional posture. Instead of avoiding difficulty, the learner seeks it deliberately.

Curiosity replaces self-judgment. Progress accelerates because attention moves to the edge of competence rather than retreating to comfort.

Learning speed is also governed by emotional tolerance. Discomfort is unavoidable in growth. Early stages feel clumsy because neural pathways are undeveloped. This discomfort is often mistaken for incapacity. In reality, it is evidence that learning is occurring. Those who progress quickly are not more confident; they are more patient with awkwardness. They understand that fluency follows friction. Emotional resilience is therefore not separate from learning—it is a learning skill itself.

Time alone does not produce competence. Quality of attention determines return on effort. Unfocused practice—performed while distracted, multitasking, or disengaged—yields shallow gains. Focused attention, even in small doses, produces disproportionate results. Protecting attention requires environmental design: minimizing interruptions, setting clear time boundaries, and committing to single-task engagement. Fragmented attention produces fragmented learning.

Another powerful accelerator is reflection. Learning does not end when practice stops. It consolidates when experience is interpreted. Brief reflection after practice—asking what worked, what failed, and what to try next—turns activity into insight. Writing these reflections deepens the effect by externalizing thought. Over time, patterns emerge. The learner begins to see not only what they are learning, but how they learn best.

Social context can either amplify or inhibit learning. Supportive environments normalize effort, reward curiosity, and treat error as expected. Competitive or judgmental environments often suppress experimentation. Learning thrives where feedback is specific and respectful. While solitary learning can be effective, carefully chosen peers, mentors, or instructors accelerate progress by exposing blind spots and alternative strategies. The key is alignment: shared goals, constructive norms, and psychological safety.

Resource selection also matters. More information is rarely the solution. Better information is. Targeted resources aligned with specific sub-skills prevent confusion and cognitive overload. Poorly curated inputs slow learning by introducing conflicting models or unnecessary complexity. Effective learners choose resources that clarify action, not merely explain theory.

Identity exerts a quiet but powerful influence. People act in accordance with how they see themselves. Statements like "I'm not technical" or "I'm bad at languages" become self-fulfilling constraints. Shifting identity language from fixed traits to active processes—"I'm learning," "I'm practicing," "I'm developing"—creates behavioral permission. Identity becomes a support for effort rather than a barrier to it.

Micro-goals strengthen this identity shift. Large goals intimidate; small, concrete milestones energize. Achievable targets provide early evidence of competence and counter narratives of inadequacy. These early wins are not trivial. They recalibrate belief through experience, which is far more persuasive than affirmation.

Learning also benefits from variation and interleaving. Alternating between related sub-skills strengthens adaptability and mirrors real-world use. This contrasts with rigid repetition, which can produce fragile competence. Variation forces retrieval and comparison, deepening understanding and transfer.

Underlying all of these principles is one unifying truth: learning accelerates when it is treated as a system rather than a test of worth. What appears to be talent is often just sustained exposure to feedback. What appears to be genius is often comfort with uncertainty and patience with repetition. Skills are not acquired through waiting to feel ready; readiness emerges through action.

The method is straightforward, though not easy: break the skill down, learn enough to correct yourself, remove friction, practice deliberately and consistently, seek feedback, reflect honestly, protect attention, and shape identity and environment to support growth. None of these steps requires extraordinary ability. They require willingness.

The deeper implication extends beyond skill acquisition. Learning well changes how a person relates to the world. It replaces passivity with agency, fear with curiosity, and limitation with possibility. When learning becomes a practiced capability rather than a rare event, life itself becomes more flexible.

There is no final ceiling to this process. The limits most people experience are not imposed by intelligence or age, but by belief and design. When belief shifts and design improves, learning expands. The mind is not fixed. It is trainable. And when trained deliberately, it learns faster than fear would ever allow you to imagine.

End of the Chapter

Chapter-13.
The Inner Axis of Leadership — How Purpose Becomes the Engine of Lasting Influence

This chapter explores how lasting influence is built from the inside out. It shows why purpose—clearly understood and consistently embodied—becomes the hidden engine of leadership that people choose to follow. By examining how belief, identity, and meaning shape commitment, the chapter offers a framework for influence that endures beyond authority, charisma, or circumstance.

Across every domain of human life, influence follows a recognizable but often misunderstood pattern. In families, some voices steady conflict while others escalate it. In organizations, some leaders mobilize commitment while others rely on compliance. In societies, some figures ignite movements that endure, while others fade once authority weakens. The difference is rarely explained by position, intelligence, or even charisma alone. It rests on something more foundational: the ability to organize action around meaning.

Influence is not a performance layered on top of work; it is a consequence of coherence beneath it. People do not commit deeply to instructions or incentives in isolation. They commit to ideas that align with how they understand themselves and the world. This chapter examines the inner axis of leadership—the way purpose, belief, and identity interact to create influence that is voluntary, resilient, and self-sustaining.

At the core of enduring influence lies a simple but demanding principle: action follows meaning. Before people decide what to do, they decide who they are and what they stand for. Any message that fails to engage this deeper layer may produce agreement, but it will not produce allegiance. Influence that lasts does not begin with activity; it begins with orientation. It answers the question people rarely ask aloud but always carry silently: What does this matter in the larger story of my life?

Most communication fails because it begins at the surface. It explains tasks, features, goals, or outcomes while assuming that motivation will follow automatically. Sometimes it does—briefly. But surface-level engagement is fragile. It depends on constant reinforcement, escalating incentives, or external pressure. When conditions change, so does commitment. Meaning-driven engagement behaves differently. When people understand and accept the underlying reason for action, they generate motivation internally. The work becomes an expression of belief rather than a response to instruction.

Purpose, in this sense, is not a slogan or a branding exercise. It is an organizing belief that explains why effort is justified and why persistence matters when progress is slow. Purpose answers the question of direction before it answers the question of method. It provides continuity across change by anchoring action to values rather than circumstances. Leaders who understand this do not treat purpose as decoration; they treat it as infrastructure.

Human decision-making reflects this architecture. Long before conscious reasoning completes its analysis, emotional and identity-based judgments shape preference. People feel alignment or resistance before they articulate reasons. When communication begins with outcomes alone, it engages the rational mind but leaves identity untouched. When it begins with belief—clearly, consistently, and sincerely—it reaches the part of the mind that governs trust and belonging. This is why shared purpose feels stabilizing. It reduces ambiguity about intent and signals what will remain constant even as tactics evolve.

The difference between inspiration and manipulation becomes visible at this point. Manipulation operates by triggering short-term responses—urgency, fear, desire, or reward. It treats motivation as something to be extracted. Inspiration operates by inviting identification. It treats motivation as something to be activated. Manipulative influence must be renewed constantly; inspirational influence renews itself because it lives inside the follower rather than outside them. One creates compliance. The other creates ownership.

This dynamic can be understood spatially rather than sequentially. Influence radiates outward from an inner core. At the center lies belief—the reason for action that answers why this matters. Surrounding it are principles—the values and standards that translate belief into consistent behavior. Only at the outer layer do results appear: products, services, decisions, and visible outcomes. When communication begins at the outer layer, it feels transactional. When it begins at the center, it feels authentic. Authenticity, in this context, is not about personality; it is about alignment between belief, behavior, and expression.

Clarity of purpose does not require grandeur. It requires specificity and consistency. A purpose that attempts to mean everything means nothing. A clear purpose defines what matters most and, by implication, what matters less. This selectivity is not limiting; it is liberating. It reduces cognitive noise and guides judgment. When people understand the purpose clearly, they can make decisions independently without constant supervision. Purpose becomes a distributed decision-making system.

This is why leaders who articulate purpose well create cultures that think rather than merely execute. Team members understand not only what to do but why certain choices are preferred. Over time, this shared understanding produces coherence. Actions align across individuals without excessive coordination because they are guided by the same inner reference point. Influence becomes ambient rather than imposed.

Identity plays a central role in this process. People do not merely support purposes; they adopt them. When a belief resonates, it becomes part of how individuals define themselves. This identity shift is powerful because it changes behavior without force. People act in ways that are consistent with who they believe they are. When purpose aligns with identity, effort feels natural rather than burdensome. Sacrifice feels meaningful rather than imposed.

This mechanism operates at every scale. In organizations, employees who identify with the underlying purpose contribute creativity and resilience beyond job descriptions. In communities, shared belief sustains cooperation even under strain. In personal life, clarity of purpose simplifies choices by aligning them with values rather than convenience. In each case, influence emerges from internal alignment rather than external pressure.

The absence of clear purpose produces predictable dysfunction. Without a stable why, organizations chase trends, overreact to short-term metrics, and fragment under pressure. Individuals become reactive, measuring success by comparison rather than coherence. Communication becomes inconsistent because it lacks an anchoring belief. People sense this instability even if they cannot name it. Trust erodes not because intentions are malicious, but because direction feels arbitrary.

Purpose-driven leadership addresses this instability by providing narrative continuity. Narrative is not storytelling for entertainment; it is the structure through which humans interpret experience. A clear purpose provides a narrative frame that explains why certain choices are made, why certain trade-offs are accepted, and why persistence is justified. When leaders articulate this narrative consistently, they reduce uncertainty and invite participation. People are more willing to commit when they understand how their efforts fit into a larger story.

However, articulation alone is insufficient. Purpose must be embodied. Every decision communicates values, whether acknowledged or not. Resource allocation, responses to failure, standards of conduct, and treatment of people all signal what truly matters. When behavior contradicts stated purpose, credibility collapses. Influence cannot survive dissonance. Authentic leadership requires the discipline to align action with belief even when doing so is inconvenient.

This alignment is most visible under pressure. In moments of crisis, purpose becomes either a compass or a slogan. Leaders who have internalized their purpose use it to navigate ambiguity without panic. They adapt tactics while preserving identity. Those without such grounding oscillate between extremes, eroding confidence. Followers watch closely in these moments. Trust deepens when purpose holds.

Purpose-driven influence also extends beyond immediate authority. When belief is clear and lived, it propagates. Others adopt the language, frameworks, and values because they provide orientation in complexity. Influence becomes generative rather than dependent. This is how movements outlast founders and organizations outlive leaders. Purpose creates continuity beyond individual presence.

Importantly, discovering purpose is rarely instantaneous. It emerges through reflection, experimentation, and refinement. Many leaders clarify their purpose only after confronting failure or contradiction. Purpose sharpens through lived experience. What matters is not immediate eloquence but ongoing engagement with the question of meaning. Avoiding that question leaves influence shallow. Engaging it honestly deepens leadership.

Once purpose is clarified, decisions simplify. Strategy becomes an expression of belief rather than a reaction to pressure. Communication gains coherence. Culture stabilizes. Innovation aligns with values rather than novelty.

Purpose does not eliminate difficulty, but it provides a stable reference point for navigating it. Influence rooted in purpose respects human psychology. It acknowledges that people seek meaning before instruction, belonging before compliance, and identity before action. Leaders who operate from this understanding do not coerce behavior; they cultivate commitment. They do not demand loyalty; they earn it through clarity and consistency.

In this light, leadership is not a function of control but a practice of stewardship—stewardship of belief, narrative, and shared direction. The leader's task is not to manufacture motivation but to reveal meaning. When meaning is clear, action follows naturally.

This is the inner axis of leadership. Not the loud assertion of authority, but the quiet coherence of purpose. Not the promise of reward, but the invitation to belong to something that matters. Influence built on this foundation does not fade when circumstances change. It adapts, endures, and continues to move people long after the original voice falls silent.

End of the Chapter

Chapter-14.
Change Your Inner World—How Personal Growth Creates Wealth, Happiness, and Freedom

This chapter shows why lasting wealth, happiness, and freedom are not achieved by chasing external rewards, but by reshaping the inner world that generates every choice. It reveals personal growth as a practical discipline—one that transforms thinking, habits, and character—so life gradually aligns with intention rather than reaction, and success becomes sustainable instead of fleeting.

If you could distill a lifetime of human aspiration into a single imperative, it might be this: become more of the person you want to be. Across cultures, across eras, and across the arc of our own daily lives, we chase things – money, status, comfort, recognition – only to discover that these external achievements fill space but not meaning. The deeper, quieter truth is that wealth and happiness are not destinations at the end of a path; they are byproducts of who you become along the way. This chapter examines that insight not as a slogan but as a working philosophy, a practical way of living that reshapes not only circumstances but the inner world from which every choice arises.

When people say they want to change their lives, they often mean they want different results without different thinking, different habits, or different emotional responses. But life does not negotiate that way. It mirrors back what you bring to it. If your internal world is disorganized, reactive, or shallow, your external world will reflect the same instability. If your inner life is disciplined, curious, and grounded, your outer circumstances gradually reorganize themselves to match that structure. This is not mysticism; it is cause and effect operating quietly over time.

The most significant shift you can make is to decide that working on yourself is not something you do after your responsibilities are handled, but something you do so that your responsibilities can be handled well. Work on the mind that thinks, the character that chooses, and the habits that repeat long before you worry about optimizing outcomes. Careers rise and fall, markets fluctuate, and opportunities change shape, but the person you become determines how you respond to every one of those shifts.

People who live intentionally do not treat life as a sequence of reactions. They treat it as a field of study. They ask questions not out of insecurity but out of respect for reality. They want to know why some people grow calmer with age while others become bitter, why some build wealth steadily while others earn and lose repeatedly, why some relationships deepen over time while others decay under familiarity. These questions are not philosophical indulgences; they are practical tools. Each honest question sharpens perception, and sharper perception leads to better choices.

Understanding how life works begins with humility. You must be willing to admit that much of what you believe has been inherited uncritically—from culture, family, fear, or convenience. Growth begins when you decide that inherited assumptions are provisional, not permanent. This does not mean rejecting everything you were taught; it means testing it. The ideas that survive testing become yours. The ones that do not fall away, leaving space for better frameworks to take their place. Learning is the mechanism of that replacement. But learning, in this sense, is not passive accumulation. It is active integration. Reading without reflection becomes entertainment. Listening without application becomes noise. Observation without interpretation becomes trivia. Real learning reshapes behavior. It alters how you speak to people, how you allocate time, how you respond under pressure, how you define success. If nothing in your behavior changes, learning has not yet occurred.

Discipline is the bridge between knowledge and transformation. Not discipline as punishment, but discipline as self-respect. It is the quiet decision to honor commitments made by your better judgment rather than surrender to the mood of the moment. Discipline is what allows small, correct actions to be repeated long enough for them to compound. Without it, even the best ideas dissolve into intention.

There is an important distinction between discipline and rigidity. Discipline is adaptive; rigidity is defensive. Discipline allows you to persist while remaining open to feedback. Rigidity clings to behavior even when evidence suggests adjustment. The disciplined person is willing to change methods without abandoning principles. This flexibility is what allows growth to continue across changing circumstances.

Self-motivation grows out of clarity. When you know why you are doing something—when the reason is rooted in values rather than appearances—effort feels purposeful rather than forced. Motivation becomes less about excitement and more about alignment. You act not because you feel inspired in the moment, but because the action is consistent with the person you are becoming. Over time, this consistency builds trust with yourself, and that trust becomes a powerful source of momentum.

Humility deepens this process. It allows you to see mistakes as information rather than as verdicts on your worth. People who resist humility often stagnate because they protect their ego at the expense of growth. Humble people move faster because they are not defending an identity; they are refining a practice. They learn from younger people, from critics, from failure, and from silence. They are curious rather than threatened.

Writing is one of the most effective tools for integrating these lessons. When you write, you slow thought down enough to examine it. You notice contradictions, assumptions, and emotional undercurrents that remain invisible when ideas stay unspoken. Writing clarifies not only what you think, but why you think it. Over time, this practice develops coherence—a sense that your actions are connected to your values rather than scattered across impulses. As this inner architecture strengthens, a shift occurs almost unnoticed. Problems that once felt overwhelming become manageable. Decisions that once felt paralyzing become clearer. You begin to respond rather than react. You start to notice opportunities not because the world has changed, but because your perception has sharpened. This is how growth produces wealth—not instantly, but inevitably. You become more capable of creating value, sustaining effort, and making long-term decisions without panic.

Happiness, too, emerges from this alignment. Not as constant pleasure, but as steadiness. As the sense that your life makes sense even when it is difficult. Happiness in this form is resilient because it is not dependent on perfect conditions. It arises from competence, connection, contribution, and meaning. It grows when you know that even hardship is shaping you rather than wasting you.

Freedom is the final consequence of inner work. Not freedom from responsibility, but freedom from compulsion. Freedom from the need to prove, to impress, to escape. When your inner world is ordered, you are less governed by fear and more guided by intention. You choose rather than drift. You act rather than wait. You build rather than cope.

This is why personal development is not self-absorption; it is preparation. It prepares you to serve better, lead better, create better, and endure better. It makes you useful to others because you are no longer governed by confusion or reactivity. The more you understand yourself, the more effectively you can engage the world. There are no shortcuts to this work. But there is a rhythm to it. Learn something meaningful. Apply it in a small way. Reflect on the outcome. Adjust. Repeat. Over years, this rhythm produces a life that feels authored rather than accidental.

Change your inner world, and the outer world reorganizes itself around that change—not because life is fair, but because cause and effect are relentless. What you become determines what you can sustain. And what you can sustain determines what you are allowed to keep. This is the work of becoming. And once begun, it never truly ends—only deepens.

End of the Chapter

Chapter-15.
The Silent Blueprint of Becoming— How Temperament Quietly Engineers a Human Life

This chapter uncovers the quiet force that shapes every human life before intention ever appears: temperament. It reveals how enduring dispositions silently influence effort, emotion, and opportunity, and how true character is formed not by erasing these tendencies, but by integrating them. Readers gain a humane framework for understanding growth, responsibility, and becoming without self-conflict.

Before a person makes a single deliberate choice, before language organizes thought or values are consciously adopted, life is already underway in a particular direction. This direction is not fate, nor is it destiny carved in stone. It is inclination – a subtle, persistent orientation toward the world that precedes intention. This orientation is temperament, and it functions as the silent blueprint from which a human life is gradually engineered.

Temperament does not announce itself with drama. It does not ask permission, nor does it wait for instruction. It is present in the earliest rhythms of attention, in the speed with which emotion rises and falls, in the ease or difficulty of transition, in the threshold at which stimulation becomes overwhelm or boredom becomes restlessness. These tendencies are not learned conclusions; they are starting conditions. And though they are often invisible to the one who carries them, they exert a shaping force on every later act of becoming.

Character, by contrast, is often misunderstood as a finished product – a moral achievement earned through effort, discipline, or cultural refinement. In truth, character is not a possession but a process. It is the evolving structure that emerges as temperament repeatedly encounters reality. It is built at the intersection of disposition and demand, where internal tendencies meet external expectation. To separate character from temperament is to misunderstand both. One provides the raw material; the other provides the form.

Every human life is constructed under constraints. No one begins with unlimited emotional capacity, uniform resilience, or identical regulatory skill. Some lives are shaped by intensity – emotions arrive quickly and powerfully, requiring constant modulation. Others are shaped by steadiness – feelings emerge more slowly, sometimes requiring deliberate engagement to reach moral urgency. Neither pattern is superior. Each carries distinct strengths and distinct vulnerabilities. Character does not erase these differences; it organizes them.

In early life, temperament is revealed with striking clarity. Infants differ not only in need but in rhythm – how they sleep, how they respond to novelty, how easily they are soothed, how strongly they react to disruption. These patterns persist across time and context. They are recognized instinctively by caregivers, long before they can be measured or named. The world responds differently to each child, not because of intention, but because temperament shapes interaction. Thus, from the beginning, temperament influences not only experience, but opportunity.

As development progresses, these early interactions accumulate. A child whose emotional responses are intense may receive frequent correction or protection. A child whose reactions are muted may be granted autonomy or overlooked. Over time, such patterns solidify into expectations – about the self, about others, about what effort feels like and what comes naturally. Character begins here, not as moral reasoning, but as adaptation. The child learns how to survive within their own nervous system and within the demands of their environment.

This adaptive process continues throughout life. Temperament shapes how challenge is perceived, how stress is processed, how meaning is extracted from experience. Two individuals may face identical circumstances, yet the internal labor required to meet those circumstances differs profoundly. One may experience conflict as energizing, another as destabilizing. One may recover quickly from failure, another may carry its emotional residue for years. These differences are not failures of will. They are features of internal climate.

Understanding this reality transforms how we evaluate human effort. Moral life cannot be assessed solely by visible behavior, because the cost of that behavior is unevenly distributed. Restraint may be effortless for one and heroic for another. Courage may feel natural to one and demand sustained inner struggle from another. Character, therefore, is not best measured by outcome alone, but by proportional effort – by the degree to which a person engages responsibly with the difficulties posed by their own disposition.

This recognition has ethical weight. It invites humility in judgment and precision in responsibility. It resists the simplistic equation of ease with virtue and difficulty with weakness. When temperament is acknowledged, responsibility becomes contextual rather than absolute.

Accountability remains intact, but it is grounded in realism. The individual who works patiently to regulate impulse demonstrates character even when imperfect; the individual who coasts on natural restraint while avoiding moral engagement does not. Throughout life, temperament and culture remain in continuous dialogue. Families, schools, workplaces, and societies reward certain temperamental styles while discouraging others. Over time, individuals learn which parts of themselves are welcome and which must be concealed. Some learn to perform sociability despite exhaustion; others learn to suppress emotional expression despite intensity. These performances may produce success, but they often do so at psychological cost. Character built in opposition to temperament tends toward fragmentation rather than coherence.

True character development does not demand the erasure of disposition. It demands integration. Integration is the process by which natural tendencies are neither indulged nor denied, but guided. It requires skill – emotional regulation, attentional control, reflective judgment. These skills are learnable, but they must be taught in ways that respect starting conditions. A strategy that strengthens one temperament may overwhelm another. Uniform methods fail because human architectures are not uniform.

Adversity reveals these dynamics with particular clarity. Difficulty does not merely test character; it exposes the structure beneath it. Individuals with high emotional sensitivity may experience suffering with immediacy and depth, making them vulnerable to exhaustion – but also capable of profound empathy. Those with lower reactivity may remain composed under pressure, enabling steady action – but risk emotional disengagement. In both cases, character matures not by altering temperament, but by balancing it.

Meaning-making plays a central role in this maturation. Temperament influences how experience is narrated internally. Some individuals process life emotionally, others cognitively. Some seek relational coherence, others conceptual clarity. Character expands when individuals learn to incorporate multiple modes of understanding, enriching their inner narrative rather than narrowing it. This expansion allows adversity to become instructive rather than corrosive.

Identity itself is shaped by these repeated encounters between inclination and demand. People do not choose their identities in abstraction; they infer them from lived experience. Where effort is required, identity tightens. Where ease is found, identity relaxes. When identity becomes rigid – when temperament is mistaken for essence – growth stalls. Mature character maintains a flexible identity, one that acknowledges enduring tendencies without surrendering possibility.

Much of what is labeled as moral failure is, in fact, regulatory overload. When expectations consistently exceed capacity, strain accumulates. Irritability, withdrawal, cynicism, and self-doubt emerge – not as signs of weak character, but as signals of unsustainable demand. Character integration begins when individuals learn to distinguish between effort that builds capacity and effort that erodes coherence. This distinction transforms self-criticism into self-understanding.

Social systems bear responsibility here. Institutions that privilege narrow expressions of competence inadvertently fragment character. Those that permit differentiated contribution foster integration. Sustainability is not indulgence; it is moral design. A society that ignores temperament exhausts its people. A society that respects it preserves collective wisdom.

At the heart of this preservation lies self-regulation – not as suppression, but as adaptive modulation. Regulation involves sensing internal signals, selecting appropriate response, and recovering efficiently from disruption. Temperament affects each stage, but character determines whether these processes are cultivated or neglected. Freedom emerges not from the absence of impulse, but from the ability to choose response.

Across the lifespan, those who learn to work with their temperament develop discernment. They become selective rather than reactive, engaged rather than driven. In later life, this integration often expresses itself as quiet authority – not dominance, but coherence. Emotional intensity softens not because it disappears, but because it is held within perspective.

In the final analysis, temperament is the given, not the verdict. It defines the terrain, not the destination. Character is the long work of shaping that terrain into a livable landscape – one capable of meaning, responsibility, and connection. When temperament is understood rather than denied, character formation becomes humane rather than coercive.

The silent blueprint of becoming is always at work. Beneath visible behavior lies an architecture shaped by disposition, refined by experience, and guided by choice. To attend to this architecture is to take human development seriously – not as an idealized abstraction, but as a lived, embodied process unfolding across time. And in that attention lies the possibility of lives lived not in conflict with their nature, but in thoughtful, responsible dialogue with it.

End of the Chapter

Chapter-16.

The Invisible Sovereign— How Electricity Quietly Rewrote Power, Thought, and Civilization

This chapter traces how electricity—once a curiosity at the edges of understanding—quietly reshaped power, perception, and civilization itself. By following its transformation from mystery to infrastructure, the chapter reveals how invisible systems reorganize society, embed values into technology, and amplify human intention, reminding us that true power lies not just in capacity, but in the wisdom guiding its use.

Long before it ruled cities, animated machines, or carried thought across continents, electricity existed as a whisper at the edges of human awareness. It did not arrive announcing itself as a future sovereign. It appeared instead as interruption – a spark that startled the senses, a lightning strike that shattered certainty, a curious attraction that defied explanation. Electricity did not first present itself as useful. It presented itself as strange. And it is precisely this strangeness that delayed its dominion while quietly preparing the conditions for it.

What distinguishes electricity from many other forces is that humanity encountered it not as substance, but as effect. Fire could be touched, water contained, wind felt directly against the skin. Electricity, by contrast, announced itself only through consequences: motion without contact, light without flame, shock without visible cause. It resisted the categories through which people had long understood the natural world. For centuries, this resistance confined electricity to the margins of inquiry, a curiosity of scholars, a metaphor for vitality, a sign of hidden sympathies in nature.

The turning point did not come from sudden brilliance, but from persistence. The gradual replacement of wonder with method marked the true beginning of electricity's transformation from mystery to instrument. When observers began to assume that even the most elusive phenomena followed regular patterns, electricity entered a new intellectual climate. Repetition replaced reverence. Measurement replaced myth. The belief that nature could be interrogated – not merely admired – was revolutionary, and electricity became one of its most demanding tests.

Early investigators did not yet possess the language to describe what they observed. They borrowed metaphors from the familiar world: fluids that flowed, pressures that built, forces that leaked or discharged. These metaphors were imperfect, but they served a crucial function. They allowed thinking to advance without full understanding. Electricity was not yet mastered, but it had become discussable, comparable, and eventually predictable. Prediction, more than explanation, is the true gateway to power.

The decisive shift occurred when electricity ceased to be fleeting. As long as it appeared only in sparks and shocks, it could not be shaped into a reliable tool. The development of sustained electrical influence changed its ontological status. Electricity became continuous rather than episodic, stable rather than theatrical. This continuity allowed causality to emerge. Conditions could be controlled, variables isolated, outcomes anticipated. Electricity entered time, and in doing so, it entered history.

With continuity came intimacy. Electricity no longer acted only at a distance; it penetrated matter itself. It rearranged substances, released hidden components, and revealed relationships between forces once thought separate. The realization that electricity and magnetism were not rivals but partners marked a profound conceptual unification. Motion could generate electricity; electricity could generate motion. Energy could be transformed, transported, and multiplied. In that reciprocity lay the foundation of modern power.

This insight did more than enable machines. It redefined geography. Energy was no longer bound to place. Water could fall in one region and illuminate another. Coal could burn far from the factory it powered. Distance lost its authority. The map of civilization began to reorganize itself around networks rather than sources. Where power could flow, influence followed.

The earliest large-scale application of this new capability reshaped communication. Electrical signaling collapsed time. Messages that once required days of travel moved in moments. This acceleration altered not only logistics, but psychology. Events felt closer. Decisions demanded speed. Coordination expanded. The telegraph did not merely transmit information; it restructured expectation. The world began to feel immediate, interconnected, and increasingly synchronized.

Yet communication was only the overture. The deeper transformation occurred when electricity became a general-purpose force. To achieve this, it required systems – generators, grids, standards, maintenance regimes. Electricity demanded organization, and organization demanded governance. Choices about voltage, distribution, and access were never purely technical. They encoded economic priorities and social hierarchies into physical form. Infrastructure became policy made durable. Illumination was electricity's most visible conquest. Darkness, once an unquestioned boundary, receded. Nights extended. Cities acquired a second life after sunset. This transformation altered labor, leisure, and safety, but it also reshaped time itself. Life no longer followed the sun. Productivity decoupled from natural cycles. Availability became continuous. What appeared as convenience carried long-term consequences for rest, attention, and expectation.

Industry felt the impact even more deeply. Electric power liberated production from centralized mechanical systems. Motors could be placed where needed, processes rearranged, scale expanded. Work became modular. Efficiency increased, but so did abstraction. Labor was reorganized around systems rather than crafts. Skill shifted from physical endurance to coordination and oversight. Electricity did not merely speed production; it redefined what work meant.

As electrification entered domestic life, it promised relief and control. Appliances transformed household labor, compressing time and effort. Yet this convenience introduced dependence. As homes filled with electrical devices, the absence of power became disruptive rather than inconvenient. Electricity transitioned from enhancement to necessity. Its invisibility signaled success, but also vulnerability. When systems fail, what was unnoticed becomes indispensable.

Alongside material change came professionalization. Electrical expertise became formalized, credentialed, and institutionalized. Universities, industries, and standards bodies formed a new ecosystem of knowledge. This stabilized progress but also concentrated authority. Electricity moved from the hands of enthusiasts into the domains of specialists. Understanding became layered: deep for some, opaque for most. Power shifted accordingly. This concentration exposed a central tension: efficiency versus resilience. Large, centralized systems optimized delivery but magnified risk. Failures cascaded. Blackouts taught harsh lessons about fragility. Over time, redundancy and regulation emerged as responses, embedding caution into design. Electricity's history became a dialogue between expansion and restraint, ambition and responsibility.

Electrification also magnified inequality. Regions connected early surged ahead; others lagged. Access to power became access to opportunity. In response, electricity was reframed as a public necessity rather than a private luxury. This shift altered the relationship between citizens and infrastructure. Power became a civic obligation, and its distribution a matter of justice.

As systems matured, electricity entered a subtler phase. It learned to carry information with precision. Signals became symbols. Patterns replaced force. Electricity began to speak. This transition transformed it from a source of energy into a medium of meaning. Control, coordination, and knowledge now flowed through currents as readily as light and motion.

With this shift came abstraction. Operators no longer touched machines; they read indicators. Responsibility migrated from sensation to interpretation. Judgment became analytical rather than tactile. Electricity demanded attention rather than strength. It trained a new kind of human operator, one who governed systems through symbols rather than force.

As networks expanded, standards became global. Compatibility replaced improvisation. Decisions made in committees quietly shaped decades of technological possibility. Paths were opened or closed not by dramatic invention, but by agreement. Infrastructure became destiny disguised as specification.

The success of electricity rendered it invisible. It faded into the background of daily life, noticed only when absent. This invisibility bred complacency. Few questioned sources, limits, or consequences. Electricity became assumed, like gravity. Only disruption restored awareness, revealing how deeply expectations had shifted.

Electricity also compressed time and space. Feedback loops tightened. Decisions accelerated. Markets reacted instantly. Governance extended its reach. Private life filled with interruption. Patience became scarce. The current recalibrated not only machines, but attention itself.

As control grew more precise, focus shifted inward. Charges within materials became manipulable. Electricity could be shaped at microscopic scales. Components shrank. Capability grew. Entire systems condensed into personal devices. What once filled rooms now fit in pockets. Complexity increased as visibility decreased.

This miniaturization intensified dependence and opacity. Fewer understood how systems worked. Repair gave way to replacement. Knowledge concentrated upstream. Electricity, once democratizing, now participated in new hierarchies of control. Yet countercurrents persisted. Education, tinkering, and open exploration preserved the idea that understanding remained possible – and necessary.

Environmental consequences eventually demanded recognition. Electricity's sources reshaped landscapes and climates. Benefits could no longer be separated from costs. Sustainability entered the narrative, not as moral ornament, but as necessity. Efficiency, alternative generation, and systemic redesign emerged as priorities. Once again, electricity absorbed new values into technical form.

When electricity became a medium of calculation, another quiet revolution unfolded. Machines learned to follow rules with perfect consistency. Workflows reorganized around reliability rather than judgment. Authority embedded itself in systems. Memory externalized. Minds shifted from recall to interpretation. Knowledge expanded, but dependence deepened.

Networks multiplied these effects. Coordination transcended presence. Control extended without proximity. Governance became systemic. Errors scaled. Models mattered as much as intentions. Electricity became a medium of administration, not just utility.

Personal life transformed alongside institutions. Constant connectivity redefined presence and absence. Identity fragmented across physical and digital spaces. Electricity enabled closeness without contact and distance without separation. Reflection followed. Calls for balance emerged, not rejecting electricity, but demanding intentional use.

Economies reorganized. Value shifted toward information and design. Work changed faster than education adapted. Global interdependence intensified. Resilience and fragility grew together. Security became perpetual adaptation rather than fixed defense.

Amid all this, electricity proved astonishingly adaptable. It carried power, signal, and thought with equal fidelity. Few forces in nature matched its versatility. As societies confronted environmental limits, electricity again stood at the center – not as problem alone, but as solution.

Local generation, storage, and participatory systems hinted at renewed democratization. Choices returned. Governance mattered. History repeated its pattern: possibilities open, structures undecided.

The invisible sovereign had arrived not through conquest alone, but through accommodation. Electricity did not dominate by force; it integrated itself so thoroughly that modern life became unimaginable without it. Its future, however, remains unsettled. Capacity is no longer the question. Direction is.

Electricity amplifies intention. It reflects values. It rewards clarity and punishes neglect. The lesson of its history is not that mastery guarantees wisdom, but that power without reflection multiplies consequence. The silent current continues to flow, carrying with it not only energy and information, but the ethical weight of how civilization chooses to live with the forces it has learned to command.

End of the Chapter

Chapter-17. The Unbroken Current—Bruce Lee, Conversation, and the Living Mechanics of Influence

This chapter examines how Bruce Lee's quiet, unscripted conversations reveal a deeper mechanics of influence—one rooted in discipline, adaptability, and responsibility rather than performance or authority. Through his words, we explore how true influence flows from practiced coherence, cultural translation, and lived verification, offering a timeless model for learning, leadership, and authentic self-expression in a changing world.

There are moments when a life concentrates itself into a voice—when years of discipline, conflict, refinement, and conviction condense into speech that carries far beyond the instant of its utterance. Such moments do not announce themselves with ceremony. They arrive quietly, embedded in conversation, unguarded by performance. Bruce Lee's recorded reflections belong to this rare category. What endures is not the celebrity of the speaker nor the novelty of the medium, but the unmistakable quality of attention in his words: alert, unsentimental, grounded in practice. Listening closely, one does not hear a man selling an image; one hears a practitioner articulating a way of engaging reality.

That conversation unfolded at a threshold moment—between eras, cultures, and definitions of mastery. The older world, structured by fixed hierarchies and inherited forms, was giving way to a more fluid modernity that prized synthesis, adaptability, and self-authorship. Lee stood squarely at that junction. His voice carried the tension of someone who had mastered traditions deeply enough to challenge them honestly. He did not reject lineage; he refused confinement. What he offered was not rebellion for its own sake, but a disciplined argument for responsiveness as the highest form of respect—respect for reality as it actually is, not as doctrine insists it must be.

At first encounter, Lee's presence appears deceptively simple. Lean, composed, quick-witted, he lacks theatrical excess. Yet beneath that economy lies density: years of training, cultural negotiation, and internal confrontation. He speaks of movement as language—not metaphorically, but structurally. A stance is a sentence. A strike is a verb. Timing is syntax. Meaning emerges not from ornamentation but from precision. In framing martial practice this way, he invites a radical reorientation: the body is not an instrument to display form, but a medium to express truth. Technique exists to communicate intent under pressure, not to preserve aesthetic purity.

This insistence on expression over imitation places Lee at odds with systems that confuse tradition with repetition. He repeatedly returns to a simple provocation: if a method no longer serves function, why preserve it?

The question unsettles because it exposes the emotional investments embedded in technique. Forms often carry identity, belonging, and status. To question them feels like betrayal. Lee's refusal to sanctify form without function is therefore not merely technical; it is ethical.

It asks practitioners to choose honesty over comfort, relevance over reverence. The phrase most closely associated with him—"be like water"—has traveled so widely that it risks obscuring its original force. Detached from context, it can sound like a plea for softness or indecision. In Lee's usage, it meant neither. Water adapts because it must. It yields where resistance would be wasteful, and it strikes where pressure concentrates. Its flexibility is not weakness; it is efficiency shaped by reality. Crucially, water retains coherence. It does not dissolve into formlessness. The metaphor, properly understood, compresses an entire pedagogy: structure must be internalized so fully that it no longer restricts response.

What often goes unnoticed is how demanding this position is. Flexibility is not a natural temperament; it is a cultivated capacity. It emerges only after repetition has disciplined instinct, after form has been absorbed deeply enough to be released. Lee was explicit about this sequence. Spontaneity without foundation is chaos. Freedom without discipline is indulgence. Only through sustained practice does responsiveness become trustworthy. In this sense, his philosophy resists both authoritarian rigidity and careless improvisation. It insists on a narrow passage between extremes.

The interview also reveals Lee's acute awareness of cultural distortion. He speaks plainly about stereotypes—not as abstract injustices, but as lived constraints. Casting expectations, audience assumptions, and market calculations pressed him toward caricature. His refusal to comply was strategic as much as moral. He understood that representation shapes possibility. To accept flattening was to collaborate in it. His insistence on being seen first as a human being was not naïve universalism; it was a deliberate counter-move against systems that profit from simplification.

Teaching occupies a central place in his reflections. Lee describes instructing actors not to manufacture spectacle, but to cultivate bodily truth. Performance, in his view, must originate from coherence between intention and movement. Emotion does not decorate motion; motion reveals emotion. This reversal undermines much conventional acting pedagogy, which often treats the body as a tool for displaying feeling rather than a site where feeling is generated and regulated. Lee's approach demands patience. It requires the actor to confront tension, imbalance, and fear directly, without shortcut. Mastery, here, is integrity under observation.

Context sharpens the significance of these ideas. Filmed in the early 1970s, the conversation captures Lee at a precarious moment. He had proven himself in Hong Kong cinema and stood on the edge of broader international recognition. Hollywood interest was present but conditional, shaped by caution and prejudice. His life would end abruptly only two years later, lending the interview a retrospective poignancy. Yet even without that knowledge, one senses a man weighing choices that carried weight beyond personal ambition. He was negotiating not only a career, but the terms under which entire traditions and identities might be seen.

One of the interview's most striking qualities is its restraint. There is no sermonizing, no grand theory announced with flourish. Lee speaks through demonstration, example, and refusal. He declines to turn his insights into doctrine. This refusal is instructive. It signals confidence without closure, authority without domination. In a culture increasingly addicted to declarative certainty, such restraint reads as radical. It suggests that understanding grows not through proclamation, but through engagement.

Synthesis emerges as a recurring principle. Lee challenges sectarian loyalty within martial arts, arguing that effectiveness, not ancestry, must guide selection. This position destabilizes institutions built on purity and lineage. Yet it also opens space for innovation and cross-cultural creativity. His relativism is not nihilistic; it is functional. It asks not "Where does this come from?" but "What does this do?" In doing so, it reframes knowledge as provisional and practice as evidence-based.

The reach of these ideas extends far beyond combat. When applied to learning, leadership, or creative work, Lee's method becomes a discipline of continuous calibration. Observe carefully. Test honestly. Retain what works. Discard what does not. Remain open to revision. These habits resist stagnation without dissolving into drift. They offer a way to navigate change without surrendering coherence. That this approach continues to resonate across domains is evidence of its depth.

The rediscovery of the interview years later added another dimension. Lost recordings acquire mythic gravity, but this footage resisted myth-making by its very plainness. It complicated heroic narratives by revealing a working mind rather than a finished icon. In a cultural moment hungry for authenticity, that mattered. The interview did not confirm legend; it restored process.

Yet influence carries risk. Ideas that travel far are prone to simplification. Detached from practice, Lee's language became portable, quotable, and vulnerable. The water metaphor, stripped of its demands, softened into aesthetic advice. What was lost was the labor: the hours of repetition, the willingness to unlearn, the confrontation with ego. This dilution is not unique to Lee; it is the fate of any idea that becomes popular. The responsibility then shifts to inheritors. To admire without practicing is to betray the insight.

What preserved Lee's philosophy from total flattening was its insistence on responsibility. He placed the burden of verification on the individual. Do not believe; test. Do not imitate; investigate. This stance resists idolization. It denies refuge in authority. Influence, in this model, is not something received; it is something activated through effort.

Translation is a recurring undercurrent. Lee was a translator in the deepest sense—between cultures, disciplines, and modes of expression. Translation always involves loss and gain. Something cannot be carried across intact. Something new emerges. The interview makes this labor visible. It reveals the ethical stakes of translation: what to preserve, what to adapt, what to refuse. Lee's commitment was to function and truth, even when fidelity to those principles complicated belonging.

His reflections on failure are equally revealing. Mistakes, he insists, are not indictments but information. They mark the edge of understanding. This stance reframes ambition. Greatness is not arrival; it is persistence in refinement. Humility, here, is not self-effacement but accuracy—the willingness to see oneself clearly enough to improve. Violence, in his philosophy, is never romanticized. Confrontation is valued only as a teacher of clarity. Under pressure, pretense dissolves. Theory yields to consequence. In such moments, one discovers what one actually knows. Training, then, becomes a controlled environment for truth—serious enough to matter, safe enough to learn. This balance mirrors his broader ethic: risk enough to grow, not enough to destroy.

As Lee's visibility grew, he faced the danger of becoming a symbol. Symbols simplify; they fossilize living practices into static images. For someone whose entire philosophy resisted rigidity, this posed a paradox. His response was to redirect attention away from himself and toward method. He spoke not of who he was, but of what one could do. This orientation safeguarded the vitality of his ideas even as it limited their commodification.

Time has only sharpened their relevance. Modern life intensifies the very tensions Lee identified: rigidity versus responsiveness, speed versus awareness, identity versus adaptability. The ability to remain flexible without fragmentation has become increasingly rare. His insistence on integration—of mind and body, discipline and freedom, tradition and innovation—addresses this predicament directly.

At a psychological level, his approach anticipates contemporary understandings of regulation and attention. Control is not suppression; it is alignment. Emotion is not an enemy; it is information. Fear, anger, tension—each signals something real. The task is not to eliminate them, but to respond with precision. This subtlety distinguishes his discipline from authoritarian models that prize obedience over understanding.

Beneath all of this lies a moral stance that is easy to miss because it is never announced. Responsibility cannot be outsourced. Tradition does not absolve judgment. Charisma does not replace effort. Each individual must test, choose, and revise.

This demand is empowering precisely because it is uncomfortable. It offers no shelter in collective certainty. Growth, in this model, is ongoing and personal.

When the voice finally falls silent, the work does not end. Ideas continue their journey—through admiration, distortion, application, and renewal. Bruce Lee's influence endures not because of slogans, but because of structure. He offered not answers, but a way of approaching answers responsibly. The wave did not break because it was never meant to crash; it was meant to flow, reshape, and continue—carrying with it the quiet demand that those who invoke it do the work it requires.

End of the Chapter

Chapter-18.
The Sovereign Within—Discipline, Self-Mastery, and the Hidden Architecture of a Directed Life

This chapter explores discipline and self-mastery as the hidden architecture behind any life lived by choice rather than habit. Moving beyond punishment and willpower, it reveals how attention, identity, emotion, and structure quietly govern behavior. Readers discover how inner order creates real freedom, sustained agency, and a sense of authorship over one's life.

There is a quiet turning point in every reflective life when a person recognizes that the most decisive forces shaping their future are not external events, social pressures, or sudden opportunities, but the unseen patterns governing their own responses. This realization rarely arrives with spectacle. It emerges gradually, often in the aftermath of disappointment, in the repetition of unkept promises, or in the subtle discomfort of knowing that one's days are being steered less by conscious choice than by habit. At this point, discipline and self-mastery reveal themselves not as moral ornaments, but as structural necessities. They are the internal architecture upon which any deliberate life must be built.

Discipline is commonly portrayed as severity—an iron rule imposed upon unruly desire, a constant struggle between what one wants and what one must do. This image is both misleading and incomplete. Discipline, in its mature form, is not antagonistic toward the self. It is cooperative. It represents an agreement between intention and action, a form of inner governance in which present behavior is aligned with long-term purpose. Self-mastery is the deeper skill that sustains this agreement. It does not eliminate desire; it educates it. Together, discipline and self-mastery create an internal order that allows freedom to function without collapsing into chaos.

At its psychological foundation, discipline begins with attention. The human mind is not naturally inclined toward consistency. It is drawn toward novelty, comfort, and immediate relief, not because it is weak, but because it evolved to respond quickly to changing conditions. In earlier environments, these tendencies were protective. In modern life, they often undermine continuity and depth. Discipline does not wage war against these impulses. It learns their language. Self-mastery begins when impulses are recognized as messages rather than mandates.

The earliest expression of discipline is not force, but awareness. Before behavior can be guided, it must be seen. Much of human action occurs automatically, driven by cues and conditioned responses. Fatigue invites avoidance. Stress invites distraction. Anxiety invites postponement. Discipline inserts a pause into this chain—a moment of observation in which response is no longer inevitable. This pause is not accidental. It is trained. Each time a person notices an urge without immediately obeying it, the capacity for self-regulation strengthens. Over time, this space between impulse and action becomes more stable, more reliable, and more humane.

Self-mastery is often confused with emotional suppression, yet the opposite is true. It requires emotional accuracy. A person who governs themselves well does not feel less; they feel more precisely. They can differentiate between fleeting impulses and enduring values, between passing moods and guiding principles.

Emotion, from this perspective, is not an enemy of discipline but a source of information. Fear may signal uncertainty, frustration may signal misalignment, desire may signal an unmet need. The undisciplined mind obeys emotion reflexively. The disciplined mind listens, interprets, and decides.

A central psychological tension underlying discipline lies between the present self and the future self. The present self seeks ease, relief, and gratification. The future self seeks stability, growth, and coherence. When discipline is absent, the present self repeatedly sacrifices the future self for momentary comfort. When discipline is present, the present self becomes a steward, acting not out of punishment or denial, but out of loyalty to what is being built. Self-mastery is the ability to hold the future with enough clarity that it can meaningfully guide the present.

This conflict is not abstract. It is embedded in the structure of the brain. Systems oriented toward immediate reward coexist with systems oriented toward planning and evaluation. Discipline is the learned capacity to allow long-term systems to guide behavior without denying the legitimacy of desire. This guidance requires repetition. Discipline is not a personality trait granted to the fortunate. It is a capacity developed through consistent use. Each small act of alignment—completing a task despite resistance, choosing rest over excess, honoring a commitment—adds strength to this internal structure.

One of the most significant insights in the psychology of discipline is that willpower alone is insufficient. Willpower fluctuates. It is sensitive to stress, fatigue, and emotional load. Self-mastery does not rely on constant exertion of force. It relies on intelligent systems. Habits, routines, and environments reduce the burden of choice by making alignment easier than deviation. When discipline is embedded in structure, it no longer feels heroic. It feels natural. Identity begins to shift. Identity plays a decisive role in sustaining discipline. People act in accordance with who they believe they are. When discipline is framed as a temporary effort, it remains unstable. When it becomes part of self-concept, it stabilizes. A person who identifies as disciplined does not argue with themselves about whether to act consistently; consistency is already assumed. This transformation does not occur through affirmation alone. It emerges when repeated actions generate evidence that the mind accepts as truth.

Failure is an unavoidable component of this process. Undisciplined minds interpret failure as proof of inadequacy and respond with avoidance or harsh self-judgment. Disciplined minds interpret failure as feedback. Psychology consistently shows that learning accelerates when mistakes are approached with curiosity rather than condemnation. Self-mastery is not the absence of error; it is the capacity to recover without collapse. Each return to intention after deviation strengthens discipline more deeply than uninterrupted success ever could.

Meaning provides another essential support. Discipline disconnected from purpose becomes brittle and resented. Discipline anchored in meaning becomes sustainable. Human beings tolerate effort far more readily when they understand why it matters. When daily practices are linked to a larger narrative—growth, service, integrity, or contribution—discipline transforms from deprivation into participation. It becomes a way of honoring what one values rather than denying what one wants.

Emotion regulation is central to this transformation. Many lapses in discipline arise not from laziness, but from unmanaged emotional states. Stress narrows perspective. Anxiety accelerates avoidance. Fatigue weakens impulse control. A mature approach to discipline includes care for the nervous system. Rest, reflection, and emotional processing are not indulgences; they are structural supports. A depleted mind cannot govern itself well. Self-mastery includes the wisdom to restore as well as to persist.

The social context in which discipline develops also matters. Humans are shaped by norms, expectations, and examples. Environments saturated with distraction make discipline costly. Environments that normalize focus and responsibility make it easier. Self-mastery does not require isolation, but it does require selectivity. Choosing influences deliberately—people, media, rhythms—is itself an act of discipline.

As discipline matures, it reshapes the experience of time. Undisciplined living fragments time into reactions. Disciplined living integrates time into continuity. Past experience informs present action, and present action serves future intention. This integration produces a sense of authorship over one's life. Agency deepens not because life becomes predictable, but because responses become intentional.

At its highest expression, self-mastery becomes ethical. It governs not only personal outcomes but interpersonal conduct. Emotional regulation influences how one speaks, listens, and responds under pressure. A disciplined individual is less reactive, less governed by momentary anger or insecurity. This steadiness fosters trust. Self-mastery thus extends beyond the self into the social fabric, contributing to collective stability.

It is a common myth that disciplined people are rigid or joyless. In reality, self-mastery expands freedom. When impulses no longer dictate behavior, choice becomes broader, not narrower. Pleasure becomes intentional rather than compulsive. Rest becomes restorative rather than evasive. Discipline protects joy by preventing it from being consumed by excess.

The development of discipline is rarely linear. Progress and regression alternate. This oscillation is not failure; it is adaptation. The psyche tests limits, recalibrates effort, and renegotiates meaning. Self-mastery matures when one abandons the expectation of permanent motivation and commits instead to consistent direction. Discipline is less about intensity than continuity.

Under pressure, the true function of discipline becomes visible. When motivation fades and emotions swell, discipline reveals itself as orientation rather than effort. It does not eliminate inner conflict; it organizes it. Resistance is natural. Every meaningful act of self-regulation generates friction. Self-mastery involves learning to interpret resistance not as a signal to stop, but as evidence that growth is occurring.

A crucial distinction must be made between discipline and coercion. Coercion relies on fear, guilt, or self-contempt. It may produce short-term compliance, but it erodes internal trust.

Discipline grounded in self-mastery operates through respect and understanding. It persuades rather than punishes. The internal dialogue shifts from "I must" to "I choose, because this aligns with who I am becoming." This shift is not cosmetic; it determines sustainability.

Delayed gratification, often simplified, is central here. It is not merely the ability to wait, but the ability to make the future emotionally present. The mind prioritizes what feels real. Discipline sharpens future representation, allowing long-term outcomes to compete with immediate temptation. Reflection reinforces this process by converting experience into insight.

Self-trust emerges gradually. Each kept promise strengthens credibility. Each broken one weakens it. Discipline is rebuilt through small, reliable commitments consistently honored. Confidence arises not from grand resolutions but from dependable follow-through.

The body remains an indispensable partner. Hunger, exhaustion, and chronic stress undermine regulation. A disciplined mind respects physiological limits. Care for the body is not separate from self-mastery; it is foundational to it.

As discipline refines desire, superficial impulses lose their urgency. Deeper longings gain clarity. This is one of self-mastery's paradoxes: by limiting excess, it expands satisfaction. Imagination, when grounded, supports this process by making consequences vivid rather than abstract.

Boredom presents another test. Many abandon discipline when novelty fades. Yet boredom tolerance predicts long-term success. Discipline transforms boredom into a training ground for focus and resilience.

Ultimately, self-mastery converges on a demanding truth: freedom is not the absence of structure, but the presence of self-governed structure. Without discipline, impulses rule. With discipline, values lead. This governance does not promise control over outcomes; it promises integrity in action.

As the inner architecture stabilizes, life becomes clearer rather than easier. Choices align more readily with intention. Regret diminishes as learning accelerates. Thought, emotion, and action begin to move in the same direction. Energy once consumed by inner conflict becomes available for creation and contribution.

This is the quiet power of self-mastery. It does not seek recognition. Its rewards are subtle and enduring: self-respect, clarity, and the knowledge that one's life is being shaped deliberately rather than accidentally. In a world that profits from distraction and surrender, discipline stands as an act of inner sovereignty—a daily decision to govern oneself with intelligence, compassion, and purpose.

End of the Chapter

Chapter-19.
The Silent Syntax of Justice—Nelson Mandela and the Discipline that Sustains Freedom

This chapter explores how Nelson Mandela sustained freedom not through force or triumph, but through disciplined restraint, humility, and moral clarity. It reveals justice as a practiced structure—maintained by self-mastery, institutional patience, and responsibility after victory. Readers gain insight into how inner discipline transforms power into service and keeps freedom alive long after struggle ends.

Some lives do not command attention through volume or spectacle. They shape history through steadiness – through a gravity that quiets the surrounding noise and reorients others toward what matters. Nelson Mandela lived such a life. His influence did not rest primarily on oratory, charisma, or the force of victory, but on a deeper order: a disciplined inner life that governed how power was held, how suffering was interpreted, and how freedom was understood once it was achieved. To study one of his later public addresses, delivered in a moment of global recognition, is to encounter not a celebration of triumph but a lesson in moral grammar – a way of arranging thought, action, and restraint so that justice remains alive after struggle ends.

Mandela never treated honor as culmination. When standing before academic and civic audiences late in life, he consistently redirected attention away from personal achievement and toward unfinished responsibility. Political liberation, he insisted, was not synonymous with human freedom. Laws could change overnight; dignity could not. The removal of injustice was only the opening clause in a much longer sentence—one that required economic repair, educational investment, and social trust to be written patiently over generations. This refusal to confuse legal success with moral completion was not rhetorical modesty; it was disciplined realism. Mandela understood that freedom without structure decays into disappointment, and celebration without responsibility becomes betrayal.

What enables a person to speak with such restraint after decades of sacrifice? How does one emerge from confinement without becoming captive to grievance? How does authority remain service rather than entitlement? These questions cannot be answered by personality alone. They point instead to a cultivated inner order—a form of self-mastery that precedes and stabilizes public action. Mandela's address did not argue this explicitly; it enacted it. His words functioned less as instruction than as demonstration.

At the center of this demonstration stood humility of a demanding kind. Not the humility that denies worth to attract praise, but the humility that keeps the self from eclipsing the task. Mandela consistently framed his life as one thread in a collective fabric. This orientation protected leadership from distortion. Psychologically, humility operates as a stabilizer: it prevents the gradual slide from responsibility into entitlement, from service into self-preservation. Leaders anchored in humility remain teachable. They listen across disagreement, revise without humiliation, and remain accountable beyond their own image. In Mandela's case, humility was not performative; it was forged through years in which arrogance would have been both dangerous and corrosive. Equally instructive was his disciplined attention to inequality. Mandela resisted the temptation—so common after political victory—to declare the struggle complete. He named, with clarity, the material divisions that continued to wound daily life: poverty, unemployment, educational disparity, and global imbalance. This capacity to hold progress and deficiency in view simultaneously reflects a mature moral imagination. True justice does not simplify reality to protect a narrative of success. It tolerates complexity and accepts that freedom must be measured not only by rights proclaimed but by lives made livable.

The language Mandela chose mattered. He avoided theatrical excess and spoke with deliberate simplicity. This was not an absence of passion but a disciplined form of it. His tone invited participation rather than obedience. In doing so, he modeled a form of collective impulse regulation. Societies emerging from injustice often face a volatile mix of anger, hope, and urgency. Mandela acknowledged these forces without yielding to them. Rather than satisfying the emotional appeal of retaliation, he consistently oriented action toward outcomes that could endure. Such restraint is often misread as weakness. In truth, it requires an inner steadiness far stronger than aggression.

This steadiness was anchored in a future-oriented identity. Mandela's sense of self did not depend on immediate reward or recognition. It rested on a long moral horizon—the conviction that dignity must outlast any individual life. When identity is rooted this deeply, sacrifice becomes intelligible. Discomfort loses its power to dominate judgment. Mandela used memory not to imprison his audience in grievance, but to orient them toward responsibility. History, for him, was not a weapon but a resource—a place where future obligation could take root.

Yet Mandela was never naïve about the limits of personal virtue. He understood that freedom, if it is to survive, must be institutionalized. Charisma cannot substitute for constitutions.

Moral intention cannot replace durable systems. Laws, schools, courts, and economic frameworks must embody the values a society claims to hold. His call for reconstruction was therefore practical rather than sentimental. It demanded patience—the patience to build institutions whose full benefits might only appear long after one's own authority had passed. This is discipline at a civic scale.

Gratitude occupied a quiet but essential place in his moral vocabulary. Mandela acknowledged international solidarity not as dependence but as shared humanity. This form of gratitude is discerning. It accepts help without surrendering agency. Psychologically, gratitude widens perspective. It loosens the grip of grievance and makes collaboration possible. Diplomatically, it transforms assistance into partnership and memory into mutual responsibility.

His treatment of failure offers another lesson in self-mastery. Mandela did not present the democratic transition as flawless or inevitable. He acknowledged misjudgments and ongoing difficulties while refusing despair. This capacity—to confront limitation without surrendering purpose—is resilience in its mature form. Self-mastery does not require denial of error; it requires the courage to integrate error into learning. Failure becomes refinement rather than verdict.

Mandela's authority emerged not from performance but from endurance. Years of sacrifice, the willingness to bear consequences, and the consistency between word and deed formed the basis of his credibility. Authority grounded in such labor invites trust because it is perceived as earned. It reminds us that lasting influence flows less from spectacle than from alignment—between values professed and actions sustained over time. Even symbolism was handled with discipline. Ceremonies and honors were treated as instruments, not destinations.

Mandela used visibility to educate rather than to glorify. By redirecting attention from personal acclaim to shared obligation, he transformed symbolic moments into opportunities for moral formation. This is strategic restraint at its highest level: the ability to use power without being consumed by it.

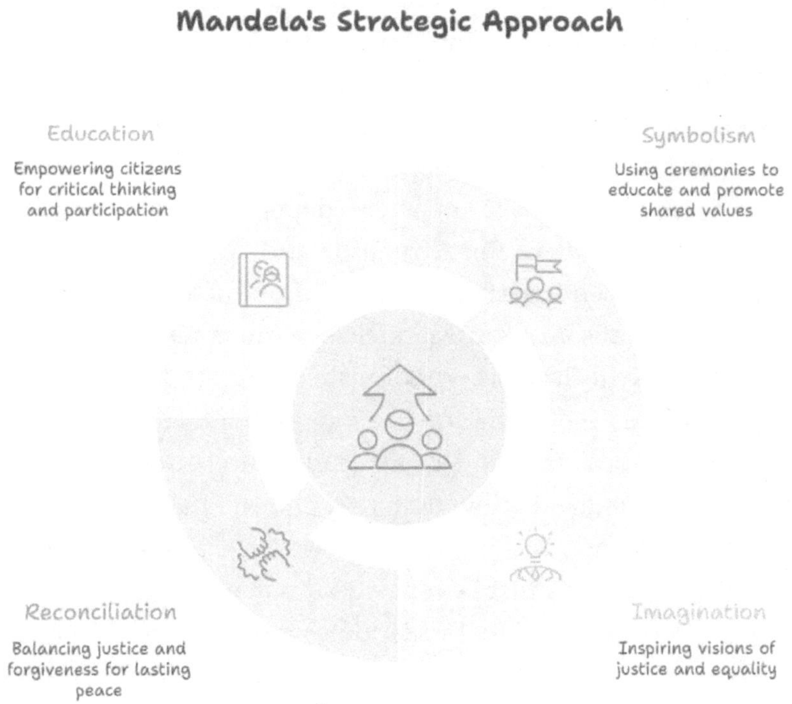

A disciplined imagination animated his vision of justice. He invited audiences to imagine societies where rights are matched by responsibilities, where economies serve human need, and where global relations are shaped by equity rather than domination. This imagination was not utopian fantasy. It was tethered to realism and translated into achievable steps. Disciplined imagination sustains perseverance by making long-term effort emotionally intelligible. It gives direction to sacrifice and coherence to planning. Reconciliation, as Mandela practiced it, was neither sentimental nor evasive. It demanded truth, accountability, and structural reform. Forgiveness without justice erases harm; justice without reconciliation perpetuates conflict. Navigating this tension requires exceptional self-governance: the ability to restrain personal anger in service of public peace, and to design processes that convert moral intention into civic stability.

Education held a central place in this vision. Mandela understood it as the foundation of freedom because it equips individuals to think critically, participate responsibly, and imagine alternatives to inherited limitation. Psychologically, education is disciplined hope—a long investment in capacities that enable autonomy. Democracies depend not only on votes, but on citizens capable of self-regulation and judgment. Educational policy, in this sense, becomes moral infrastructure.

Notably absent from Mandela's posture was triumphalism. He refused to declare the work finished. Victory over injustice, he argued, is only the beginning of a longer moral labor. This refusal of complacency functioned as leadership discipline. It kept attention on renewal rather than rest, on responsibility rather than reward. Freedom, in his grammar, was not a destination but a practice—one that must be renewed by each generation.

In personal conduct, Mandela modeled restraint under temptation. Power offers subtle seductions: favoritism, retaliation, accumulation. He countered these through relational discipline—consultation, constitutional limits, and principled decision-making. Self-mastery in public life thus appears not as solitary willpower, but as a network of practices that distribute responsibility and preserve integrity.

Perhaps most expansive was his insistence that justice is never purely local. Mandela linked the fate of his own nation to the wider human condition, arguing that persistent inequality anywhere diminishes freedom everywhere. This cosmopolitan ethic requires disciplined humility and disciplined solidarity. It calls for cooperation rooted in respect rather than charity, partnership rather than control.

Taken together, his address forms not a single argument but a curriculum in moral practice. It teaches that freedom is cultivated through habit, that justice requires inner discipline and outer design, and that leadership is shaped through patience, memory, and imagination. For individuals, the lessons are intimate: guard humility so success does not hollow character; anchor action in story so effort acquires meaning; use recognition as responsibility; and build structures that sustain values beyond personal strength.

For societies, the message is equally clear. Reconstruction demands honesty about inequality, sustained investment in education, accountable institutions, and reconciliation treated as long labor rather than emotional gesture. These are slow processes. They require the kind of endurance Mandela embodied.

Ultimately, this chapter invites moral rehearsal. To study such a life is to be invited into its posture: attentive to injustice, resistant to resentment, committed to institutions that outlast individuals, and courageous enough to imagine inclusive futures. Self-mastery here is not withdrawal from the world, but deeper participation in it. Discipline becomes the means by which freedom is preserved, and mastery becomes service rather than domination. In learning this silent syntax, one does not merely admire justice from afar—one begins, quietly and persistently, to practice it.

End of the Chapter

Chapter-20.
The Hidden Atlas of Self-Command Discipline, Desire, and the Art of Living Deliberately

This chapter reveals discipline as an inner map rather than a rigid rulebook—a way of understanding impulse, desire, and choice with clarity and care. It shows how self-mastery transforms reaction into authorship, refining pleasure instead of denying it. Readers learn how deliberate structure, meaning, and compassion combine to create a life guided by intention rather than drift.

Inside every human life lies a terrain rarely charted with care. It is not a place of roads and borders, but of tendencies and thresholds – of impulses that rise like sudden winds, of habits that form valleys worn by repetition, of intentions that stand like distant peaks, visible yet difficult to reach. Most people move across this inner landscape by habit alone, following familiar routes without reflection, surprised when they arrive at destinations they never consciously chose. Discipline is the practice that interrupts this drift. It is the skill of mapping the inner world with honesty, learning its patterns, and choosing one's direction with intention. Self-mastery is not a single triumph on this map; it is the lifelong craft of reading it accurately and traveling it well.

Discipline is often reduced to a checklist of behaviors: wake early, work consistently, resist temptation, keep promises. These actions matter, but they are surface expressions of something deeper. Beneath every disciplined act lies a psychological structure—a way of relating to impulse, time, effort, and meaning. Without understanding that structure, discipline becomes fragile. It relies too heavily on willpower, collapses under stress, and is experienced as deprivation rather than freedom. True discipline begins not with command but with comprehension.

The human mind is not designed for long horizons by default. It is tuned to immediacy: to the quick reward, the familiar comfort, the rapid escape from discomfort. This bias is not a defect; it is an inheritance. For most of human history, attending to what was immediate and tangible ensured survival. In modern life, however, the same bias often undermines pursuits that require patience—learning a craft, sustaining relationships, building health, or shaping a meaningful career. Discipline begins when this mismatch is recognized. Impulses are no longer treated as enemies to be crushed, nor as authorities to be obeyed, but as signals to be interpreted.

The most powerful tool in this interpretation is the pause. Discipline grows in the small interval between urge and action. That interval does not need to be dramatic. A single breath before speaking, a moment of awareness before opening a screen, a brief stillness before responding to frustration—these micro-pauses are acts of quiet sovereignty. They create just enough space for choice to appear. Repeated over time, they reshape neural patterns. Reactivity softens. Attention strengthens. The person who once believed themselves to be impulsive begins to experience themselves as capable of selection.

Contrary to popular belief, discipline does not narrow life; it widens it. What looks like resistance to pleasure is often protection of deeper satisfactions. Immediate indulgence tends to exhaust itself quickly, leaving little behind but repetition and regret. Disciplined action, though initially demanding, often yields layered rewards: the satisfaction of completion, the confidence of reliability, the slow joy of competence. Self-mastery does not eliminate pleasure; it refines it, preserving the capacity to enjoy without being consumed.

A pivotal shift occurs when discipline moves from behavior to identity. People do not act primarily according to what they want in a given moment, but according to who they believe themselves to be. Identity is not fixed; it is constructed through evidence. Small, repeated actions quietly rewrite self-understanding. A person becomes disciplined not by declaring it, but by performing disciplined acts until the mind accepts the pattern as truth. Goals framed as becoming—becoming a learner, a craftsperson, a reliable friend—outlast goals framed only as tasks. Identity sustains action when motivation fades.

Structure is the ally of this process. Willpower is real but finite. It is depleted by stress, hunger, and excessive choice. A disciplined life therefore relies less on constant effort and more on intelligent design. Habits automate alignment. Environments are arranged so that the desired action is the easiest one to take. This is not weakness; it is wisdom. Removing unnecessary temptation, reducing friction, and embedding routines honors human limitation while serving human aspiration.

Yet structure alone is insufficient. Discipline without meaning becomes mechanical and brittle. It fractures under pressure because it lacks emotional fuel. Human beings endure difficulty when they understand why it matters. Purpose transforms effort into participation. When daily practices are connected to values—service, growth, integrity, contribution—discipline becomes a form of self-respect rather than self-denial. The question "Why am I doing this?" is not philosophical decoration; it is psychological infrastructure. Failure, inevitably, enters the landscape. No path of discipline is uninterrupted.

Promises are broken, routines dissolve, resolve weakens. The decisive difference lies not in avoiding failure but in responding to it. Undisciplined minds treat failure as a verdict on worth and retreat into avoidance or self-attack. Self-mastery treats failure as information. It asks: What condition was underestimated? What assumption proved false? What adjustment is needed? This experimental stance transforms setbacks into refinement. Each recovery strengthens the very capacities discipline requires.

Emotion regulation is the most demanding terrain on the map. Stress, loneliness, anger, and fatigue distort judgment and narrow choice. Many lapses in discipline are not failures of character but failures of regulation. Practical psychological skills—mindful awareness, naming emotions, reframing perspective—are therefore not luxuries. They are instruments of governance. To name an emotion is to reduce its power. To reframe a challenge as growth rather than threat is to reclaim agency. These practices do not remove feeling; they make it navigable.

Self-mastery is never purely solitary. Human beings are shaped by their environments and relationships. Social contexts normalize either discipline or drift. Wise practitioners choose their influences deliberately. They cultivate relationships that mirror the virtues they seek and accept accountability as a form of support rather than surveillance. Public commitment, mentorship, and shared goals transform private intention into sustained action. Discipline flourishes when it is socially scaffolded.

Time perception plays a subtle but decisive role. Those who live only in the present make different choices than those who consult the future habitually. Discipline trains the imagination to hold long-term consequences with emotional clarity. Techniques that make the future vivid—written reflections, progress tracking, reminders of purpose—strengthen delayed gratification. The disciplined mind does not ignore the present; it integrates it into a longer arc.

Rituals provide rhythm to this arc. They mark transitions and focus attention. Simple, repeated actions signal the beginning of meaningful work and reduce the friction of starting. Rituals are not superstition; they are cognitive scaffolding. They turn intention into momentum.

Compassion is the often-missing element in discipline. Harsh self-talk may produce short bursts of compliance, but it erodes trust and increases avoidance. Sustainable self-mastery pairs firmness with kindness. Standards are held clearly, but mistakes are met with learning rather than shame. This compassionate discipline preserves morale and keeps growth possible.

Over time, discipline reshapes desire itself. Repeated restraint recalibrates appetite. Trivial pleasures lose urgency; deeper satisfactions gain clarity. Attention becomes capable of subtler joys: sustained concentration, meaningful conversation, craftsmanship, and quiet accomplishment. Discipline does not starve desire; it educates it.

Ethically, discipline is the workshop of character. Patience, prudence, fidelity, and courage are not formed in declarations but in repetition. Each small act of self-governance contributes to moral reliability. In this sense, self-mastery is not merely personal optimization; it is preparation for responsible participation in the world.

The path is best traveled incrementally. Small, manageable commitments create momentum. Gradual expansion respects the biology of change. Reflection and revision keep discipline adaptive rather than rigid. Life evolves; practices must evolve with it.

The reward of sustained self-mastery is not perfection but agency. With inner order comes the capacity to pursue what matters without constant self-interference. Freedom reveals itself not as the absence of constraint, but as the presence of self-chosen structure. Attention is stewarded rather than scattered. Energy is invested rather than leaked.

This is the quiet promise of discipline: by learning to govern the inner landscape with intelligence and care, one gains access to a wider, steadier freedom. Not the freedom of impulse, but the freedom of authorship—the ability to shape a life deliberately, to say no to what diminishes, yes to what enlarges, and to move through the inner world not as a wanderer, but as a skilled navigator.

End of the Chapter

Chapter-21.
Small Engines, Vast Horizons—Soichiro Honda and the Patient Intelligence that Set the World in Motion

This chapter explores how lasting transformation often begins with modest tools and patient minds. Through Soichiro Honda's life, it reveals a philosophy of progress built on failure, craft, and respect for reality. Readers discover how disciplined curiosity, ethical engineering, and incremental improvement can expand human freedom—quietly turning small engines into forces that reshape societies.

History often celebrates revolutions as sudden eruptions—moments when the world appears to turn on a single decision, a dramatic invention, or a charismatic declaration. Yet most enduring change moves differently. It advances quietly, powered by modest mechanisms, repeated effort, and minds willing to work patiently at the edge of failure. The life and work of Soichiro Honda belong to this quieter tradition. His story is not one of instant brilliance or inherited advantage, but of an intelligence forged through touch, error, persistence, and an unwavering respect for how things actually work. From small engines assembled under severe constraint emerged a way of thinking about progress itself—one that reshaped mobility, industry, and the daily rhythm of modern life.

Soichiro Honda did not begin with a vision of empire. He began with curiosity and necessity. Raised in rural Japan, he grew up surrounded by the practical realities of repair and reuse. His father's blacksmith shop and bicycle repairs offered a formative education in material honesty. Metal bent or broke according to laws that could not be negotiated. A wheel either turned smoothly or failed at speed. These early encounters instilled a fundamental principle that would guide Honda throughout his life: reality is the final judge of all ideas. A design that looks elegant on paper but fails under use is not a design at all; it is a hypothesis awaiting correction.

This grounding in physical reality shaped Honda's temperament as much as his skill. He developed a deep impatience with abstraction divorced from function. Formal schooling never fully satisfied him, not because he lacked intelligence, but because he learned best when theory answered to practice. When he moved to Tokyo as a teenager, he entered not a university but a living laboratory.

Workshops, garages, and racing pits became his classrooms. He watched experienced mechanics, copied them imperfectly, failed conspicuously, and tried again. Each failure sharpened his perception. Each correction refined his judgment. Over time, this cycle produced not only technical competence but a disciplined way of thinking: build, test, break, learn, rebuild.

The interwar and wartime years intensified this discipline. Japan's industrial environment during this period was unforgiving. Materials were scarce, demand unpredictable, and destruction frequent. Honda's early ventures, particularly his attempts to manufacture piston rings, were marked by rejection and loss.

Designs failed to meet standards. Facilities were damaged by bombing. For many, such setbacks would signal the end of ambition. For Honda, they clarified a crucial insight: work is not a product, but a capacity. A factory can be destroyed; a method of thinking cannot. This distinction freed him from despair. He learned to begin again without sentimentality, carrying forward only what experience had proven useful.

The aftermath of war confronted Japan with an urgent practical problem: movement. Roads were damaged, fuel limited, and conventional vehicles inaccessible to most citizens. Honda's response was neither theoretical nor heroic. It was adaptive.

By attaching small engines to bicycles, he created a form of transport that matched the country's constraints precisely.

These early motorized bicycles were simple, affordable, and repairable. They did not promise luxury or speed; they promised reliability.

In doing so, they restored a measure of agency to people whose lives had been compressed by scarcity. This act captures the essence of Honda's genius: he did not wait for ideal conditions, nor did he impose an idealized solution. He worked within reality and improved it incrementally.

As demand grew, so did the need for structure. Honda's personal brilliance alone could not sustain expansion. The partnership he formed with a complementary business mind transformed his inventions into a viable enterprise. This collaboration illustrates a vital truth often obscured by hero narratives: innovation becomes social before it becomes transformative. Ideas matter, but institutions carry them into the world. What distinguished Honda's growing company was its refusal to sacrifice engineering integrity for rapid growth. Production scaled, but standards did not dilute. Each engine was expected to perform not just once, but repeatedly, under varied conditions. Trust was built slowly, one reliable machine at a time.

Central to this culture was an uncompromising attitude toward quality. Honda was demanding, sometimes to the point of discomfort for those around him. He rejected sloppy work not as a matter of temperament, but of ethics. To him, a poorly made product was a form of deception. It betrayed the user, who depended on the machine not as an ornament but as a tool woven into daily life. At the same time, Honda fostered an unusual respect for failure. Failure, when examined honestly, was a teacher. His engineers were encouraged to test parts until they broke, not to avoid weakness, but to reveal it. Reliability, in this view, was not luck or inspiration; it was the cumulative result of confronting weakness repeatedly and refusing to ignore it.

As the company matured, it expanded cautiously but confidently. Motorcycles led naturally to automobiles. Small engines found applications in generators, agricultural equipment, and beyond. Each new domain was approached not as conquest but as translation. Skills learned in one context were adapted, tested, and refined in another. This disciplined diversification prevented the kind of overreach that has undone many ambitious firms. Growth followed competence, not speculation.

The social impact of these products extended far beyond the balance sheet. Affordable mobility altered the geometry of everyday life. People could travel farther for work, education, and trade. Rural and urban economies became more connected. Time itself was restructured, as distances once prohibitive became routine. These changes were not neutral. Increased mobility contributed to new patterns of consumption and environmental strain. Yet within these broader trends, Honda's emphasis on efficiency and durability moderated harm. Engines that consumed less fuel and lasted longer reduced waste. Design choices reflected an awareness—sometimes implicit, sometimes explicit—that technological progress carries responsibility.

This awareness became more visible as global conditions shifted. Energy crises, environmental regulations, and changing consumer expectations demanded adaptability. Rather than resisting these pressures, Honda treated them as engineering challenges. Constraints became prompts for innovation. Cleaner, more efficient engines were developed not as compromises, but as achievements. This anticipatory mindset insulated the company from shocks that crippled competitors who clung too tightly to existing models. It also demonstrated a broader principle: the most resilient technologies are those designed with future limits in mind.

Internally, Honda cultivated a distinctive organizational culture. Hierarchies were flattened where possible. Managers were expected to understand the realities of production. Designers were encouraged to spend time on the factory floor. This proximity reduced the distance between decision and consequence. Problems were identified quickly, feedback loops tightened, and responsibility remained tangible. Such an environment demands competence and humility in equal measure. Authority flowed not from title alone, but from understanding.

Global expansion tested these values. Establishing operations in new countries required more than logistical planning; it required cultural sensitivity. Honda's approach emphasized local training, respect for labor practices, and long-term investment. Rather than exporting a rigid template, the company translated its core principles—quality, learning, accountability—into diverse contexts. This adaptability allowed it to integrate into local economies rather than merely extracting value from them.

In his later years, Soichiro Honda occupied an ambiguous role. No longer responsible for daily operations, he nonetheless remained emotionally invested in the company's direction. His critiques were often pointed, reflecting his enduring attachment to craftsmanship. Yet this tension is instructive. Founders who care deeply about their creations must eventually accept that institutions evolve beyond individual control. Honda's lasting contribution in this phase was not control, but reminder. He served as a living reference point for the values that had guided the company's formation.

Ethically, Honda's legacy resists simplification. Industrial growth inevitably reshapes environments and societies. Mobility enables freedom but also accelerates consumption. Honda's life does not resolve these tensions, but it offers a model for engaging them responsibly. Choices about efficiency, durability, and learning orientation matter. They influence not only profitability, but the quality of the world technologies help create.

At a personal level, Honda's story stands as a rebuttal to myths of effortless success. His achievements accumulated through embarrassment endured, mistakes examined, and improvements repeated. Innovation, for him, was not a moment of revelation, but a habit of attention. This humility was not passive. It was strategic. It produced tools that lasted and institutions capable of adapting.

Ultimately, the measure of Honda's impact lies not in numbers alone, but in expanded possibility. The farmer reaching markets, the student commuting to education, the worker extending their range—these are the quiet outcomes of disciplined engineering. The challenge ahead is to carry this legacy forward into an era that demands mobility reconciled with environmental care and social equity.

Soichiro Honda's life illustrates a disciplined imagination: begin with what is available, learn relentlessly from failure, honor craft, and scale without forgetting responsibility. His story reminds us that the world is often moved not by those who announce the future loudly, but by those who patiently refine the present. In the steady hum of engines that power daily life, there echoes a philosophy born in small workshops—a belief that improvement, however incremental, can accumulate into transformation when pursued with integrity.

The End